MW00743855

SHRINK YOUR BODY, GROW YOUR MIND

By Lori Sawyer & Caren Boscaino

ISBN: 9781091704855

Scriptor
PUBLISHING GROUP

Do you like coffee, cream, butter,
tequila, vodka, bacon, wine?
We do, too...so we figured out a way
to enjoy them all, and still lose weight!

Table of Contents

Chapter 1

Introduction

Almost six years ago, we were two women in the same field, at the same pivot in the road, at the same stage of motherhood. Somehow we found each other. At the time we didn't know our friendship would grow into more, but eventually it became a partnership. We had different personalities and different strengths, but we had the same driving desire to help people change their lives. That is what made us a perfect team and led us to create Clean Cut Fitness & Nutrition.

Together we built our friendship through running programs and helping moms. We took our clients from some of their first 5K races all the way to half marathons.

In fact, we continue to work so well together today due to the success we've had in guiding others to identify and reach their goals and in inspiring them to create new ones.

When a group of our clients approached us and asked if we could hold a weight loss challenge, yup, another new path opened for us. Excited by this idea, we sat down and put our methods, past fitness experiences, new education, and life experiences together to design a simple but effective weight loss challenge. We decided six weeks was the ideal time to break apart some old habits and create new ones. We also knew six weeks wasn't the final answer, and a lifetime of work was needed, but we knew it was a great foundation. Clean Cut was born. This simple, one-time challenge designed for this group, worked, and as you can imagine, people started asking, "What did you do? You look great!" Word got out, and interest grew, so we went with it and ran another challenge. We tweaked things along the way, building on our foundation. When things worked, we made them better. Things that had become roadblocks, we changed.

We are always evolving and learning, which is the greatest part of Clean Cut. After our first small challenge gained momentum, we decided to create something for our clients and so many others. Over the years, Clean Cut has gone from a few challenges a year, to a national program that holds multiple core challenges along with holiday handhold programs, summer slam events and other pop-up programs that help people learn and succeed in the world of weight loss and management.

Caren's Story

I was turning sixteen years old and found running as a hobby and a tool to stay in shape. Running then led to working out at the gym, and ultimately, to what became my career. It wasn't always as easy as it looked. My desire to stay fit went from healthy to extremely unhealthy. I struggled with eating disorders on and off from age sixteen into adulthood. I was finally fed up with the cycle and lies I was living. On the surface, everything seemed normal—job, kids, home, friends. I had it all but was secretly fighting. Can you imagine how frustrating and tiring it had become? It was time to dig deep, find the reason why, and learn to trust myself and food. All I wanted was to finally have a healthy relationship with food. This is what led me back to school. I became certified through IIN (Institute for Integrative Nutrition) and other continuing education to shape and change my behaviors. I took everything I had learned about food during the previous forty years, threw it away, and began to trust and educate myself on how food really works in the body and how to be kind to myself mentally, physically, and emotionally. We all have a relationship with food, and true knowledge takes the guesswork out and makes staying the path that much easier.

Lori's Story

I have been active my entire life. I grew up playing sports, so leading a very active lifestyle came naturally to me. It was always easy to eat what I wanted and never gain weight. I was one of the lucky ones. College lifestyle got the better of me, though, and I remember trying on a dress for a formal, looking in the mirror and crying. I decided to bring the active me back—the one I missed. In that moment, my passion and love for fitness and wellness were reignited. I became a Certified Athletic Trainer and incorporated personal and group fitness into the mix to create a unique opportunity. Combining these two professions with a nutrition certification launched a new stage in my career.

My desire to win as an athlete transformed into a desire to coach individuals to help them create a successful Clean Cut Lifestyle. Growing a fitness stroller class business for local women turned into outdoor boot camps, running programs and a safe place for women to get back into shape after having children. My clients kept asking for more, so I gave them more.

The feeling I get when a client succeeds is truly second to none. Whether it's weight loss, achieving a race goal, a get up off the couch goal, or a mental goal, the Clean Cut lifestyle is about more than just food. It's about life. As a busy mom of three, I am in it with our clients. My goal is to be the best coach, mom, and friend I can be–a role model that my clients and children will look up to. The Clean Cut lifestyle makes this possible.

Shrink Your Body and Grow Your Mind in Six Weeks

Clean Cut is not just about what to eat and what not to eat. It's about real mind shifts (pivots) to create new lasting results. We wanted to design a program that took the guesswork out, something you can do for the rest of your life with room to enjoy the things you love. After years of practice, we believe we've found an answer. A series of small changes in your lifestyle will build the foundation for the rest of your life and real success. The next six weeks are the stepping stones you need to lead you to your new healthy habits. You will learn things about yourself and grow as a person, all while learning what foods to eat, how they react in your body, and how to trust them. You'll also learn shortcuts to keep you on track, tips on dining out, travel, and so much more. You will learn to make smart choices and eat around "life." We are here to guide you through real life. We never say never. There is room in life for the things you love. We teach you how to make choices around "cheats" and keep a balanced life because perfect is truly boring.

We strongly believe in the science and education of nutrition and fitness and want you to understand why things work. Anything new is easy for the first few weeks. It's when you hit week four or five and say to yourself, "OK that was fun, but now I just want…" that's when real change happens. We do not want your head to slip back to old ways. Stay with it and break the habit for real. PIVOT and see what your next level looks like!

Excited?

We are!

Welcome to the CLEAN CUT program!

CHOICES

Let's put the idea of this program's being all about food aside for a minute and talk about choices. This program is not about having control. That is something we can't have all the time. It's about CHOICES.

> CHOICE: An act of selecting or deciding when faced with two or more possibilities. Remember, you always have a choice. Today's nutrition choices can be balanced tomorrow, as long as you are clear in why you are making a specific choice.

Where does your head go when you look at your week as a whole? You have a dinner Thursday night and again on Saturday. You are aware you aren't as strict over the weekends as you said you would be, leaving you angry and having regret. Imagine having the ability to really balance your lifestyle without feeling like you are being deprived. Here is where the mindset comes in. PLAN FOR THE CRASH! Don't just say you will take care of it tomorrow, plan for it today. "Just a bite" and "only a handful" add up to significant calories over time. We want you to be so mindful that choices become easy to make. We want you to be honest with yourself and realize that every decision, good or bad, has its effect.

We've all dieted down to get into that dress or bathing suit. Why don't we plan like that for our daily life? If you know Thursday night is your date night and you know you are never perfect, get out in front of it so you are ready. If you planned on not cheating and you go off the rails, undo or erase it the next day. This is the mindset we are talking about. You can't cheat yourself or make up excuses. Your body tells the truth.

So how do we do this? Here is an example. Last weekend Lori and I went out with our guys for drinks and a bite to eat. We both knew it wasn't going to be super clean so that day we left out all carbs and fruit and saved those calories for our drinks and food choices. We got our workouts in, drank all our water with Himalayan Pink Salt, left out chocolate the day before, made good enough choices at dinner and voilà–success. Oh, and yes, running an extra mile the next day to burn off those fries was needed! Total SUCCESS and totally worth it!

When you do cheat, MAKE IT GOOD. Those small, useless bites of your kid's cold chicken fingers or soggy fries aren't worth it on any day. Remember food is energy. If you have plenty stored (from a big meal or a big cheat), you don't need to refill the tank. Try intermittent fasting the day after; eat smaller meals with just veggies, protein, and your good fats; drink lots of water; WORKOUT or workout for an extra 20 minutes to get yourself back to neutral.

The Clean Cut way of life is like no other. It's education, it's pivots, and it works. Finding what works for you may be different than what works for your bestie. THIS is why it is a lifestyle. One you can live with!

SHRINK YOUR BODY, GROW YOUR MIND

Clean Cut Fitness & Nutrition is a six-week "course" to a truly sustainable new you. Learn a healthy way of eating and mindfulness with no fad diet, no magic pill or drink, just real weight loss and life change.

We have created this six-week course over the last several years and have worked with hundreds of people, from teenagers, new moms, and husbands to empty nesters—all who have achieved proven long-term success. We want you to be able to keep the foods you love in your life while giving you the tools to lose weight, fight disease, and have overall better energy. We know there isn't one "right way" to eat, so that is why we have created a Clean Cut Toolbox full of options. With the use of different techniques, meal plan choices, and plateau busters, this program helps you create the perfect plan for your lifestyle. We are not only going to teach you what to eat but when to eat and how to cheat. We call these PIVOTS.

If you have small pivots and work on them until they become second nature, then move onto another pivot until that becomes second nature, you will make real change. Create your pivots—small changes that build your new foundation for real change in your life.

> **PIVOT:** A small change in your Clean Cut lifestyle. Making small pivots or changes one at a time helps lead to overall big change and will create a new lifestyle you can balance.

The Clean Cut program guides you through a week-one detox and sets you up for the following weeks to learn how to be successful.

This detox consists of real food, real choices, and most importantly, real life. Each week, we discuss a different topic of the clean eating lifestyle. These include eating non-GMO, eating organic (avoid the dirty dozen), emotional eating, tips for parties and travel, and how to handle negative cravings while simultaneously learning to trust your food options. Our goal is not only to teach you what to eat but to make you understand the choices you are making (good or bad) in a mindful way.

Week by week we are going to make small pivots, which will grow into new healthy habits. You will discover your safe foods and meals and start to trust your daily decisions without overthinking. Over time, this new way of thinking and eating will become second nature. Imagine what you are capable of with the proper tools and support.

WHY IS CLEAN CUT DIFFERENT?

Yes, we teach you what foods to eat. We also teach you how to enjoy your wine, tequila, cake, or whatever it is that brings joy in your life, all while guiding you to the right mindset of the choices you make around it by using your Clean Cut tools.

We have all heard "everything is good in moderation." Well, this is true. Even the good becomes bad when we overdo it. This book will also teach you portion control and how to make a healthier choice that satisfies you. Imagine feeling satisfied by not overeating. Imagine not always thinking about your next snack or meal. We teach you what combinations of foods to eat so you have balance and that sense of satisfaction so you can pause and not overeat.

With this six-week guide, you will start to look and feel different. It will be easy to continue on your path because you will not feel deprived in any way. These are not only lessons on food, but lifestyle lessons. This is Clean Cut.

You will have support from other members on Facebook, and so much more. Included in this book are clean recipes for weekly meals that you and your family will enjoy, along with recipes for treats and makeovers of old-time classics. There are vegetarian options, brand suggestions, and apps and websites we use often.

About the Authors

Lori Sawyer, MA, ATC

National Athletic Trainers Association, Certified Athletic Trainer
National Academy of Sports Medicine, Personal Trainer
National Association of Sports Nutrition, Licensed Sports Nutritionist

Lori Sawyer earned her Bachelor of Science degree in Movement Studies and Exercise Science with a concentration in Athletic Training from East Stroudsburg University in Pennsylvania. She went on to receive a Master of Arts Degree in Exercise Science from Montclair State University in New Jersey, and upon graduation, took a position at Seton Hall University as an athletic trainer for two years. She then moved to Los Angeles to become a staff athletic trainer at UCLA where she was responsible for traveling with the women's basketball team and directly responsible for training the women's tennis and 2003 NCAA national championship women's water polo teams. As an athletic trainer, Lori has focused on injury prevention, rehabilitation, and sports-specific training. She has developed a well-deserved reputation in the field for bringing athletes back from injury, quickly and safely.

Throughout her career, Lori has trained hundreds of clients from every walk of life to help them improve their lifestyle and achieve their specific goals. When her eldest son was born, she wanted to stay at home with him, but didn't want to end her professional career...so MOMMY-MOVES FITNESS was born! Now with three beautiful boys, Lori has transitioned to helping families create healthy lifestyles through fitness and nutrition. She not only founded Mommy-Moves, but also created Mommy-Runs, and Extreme Mom Boot Camp classes. Formerly a fitness columnist for the online parenting website The Family Groove, and "mom blogger" for Meridian Healthcare Systems' Meridian Momtourage website, Lori now shares her expertise as a fitness influencer for the women's apparel company. She has numerous speaking engagements under her belt, including regional athletic training conferences and Meridian events. She often holds her fitness classes at the local retail store and has filmed a stroller fitness class for an MTV reality show.

She has now jumped into building an online nutritional program with Caren Boscaino that will focus on the full infinity loop of health, wellness, and all-around mindfulness—Shrink Your Body, Grow Your Mind.

Caren Boscaino

National Academy of Sports Medicine, Personal Trainer
National Association of Sports Nutrition, Licensed Sports Nutritionist
ACE Group Fitness Instructor
Weight Loss and Health Coaching Degree through IIN
(Institute for Integrative Nutrition)

A mom of two, Caren grew up on Long Island, graduated from the C.W. Post Campus of Long Island University, and worked in advertising until she made her career switch in 2001 to her real passion—health and fitness. Her idea of fitness has changed over the past seventeen years. It's not just about the way you look, it's the entire package. Throughout her career, she has guided and challenged all types of clients to look at fitness differently which has set them on a new path to reach their desired goals and keep setting new ones. One of the favorite parts of her job is when she runs into old clients, and they tell her, "You have no idea what you did for me. I will never forget the time you said…" or "Your creativity made me try new things since we last worked together." As a fitness and health professional her goal is to help people make positive changes, and when something clicks, it makes it all worth it. She starts by suggesting clients make small changes that stick, which then leads to their setting new larger goals. In the end, she ultimately works to create a new you. With guidance in nutrition, physical activity, and mental challenges she helps her clients find balance in life because she has worked on that for herself and finally found it.

CHAPTER 2

Shrink Your Body,
Grow Your Mind

What Is Clean Cut Eating?

Rule to follow: if it comes out of a package, it's gone through a process. Yes, there are better options out there now than years ago, but packaged foods need to be kept to a minimum (portioned). If you are eating out of your refrigerator, you are most likely eating clean. Supermarkets are making it easier to eat clean these days by stocking new items from riced cauliflower to spiralized veggies. If supermarkets are getting on board, why wouldn't you?

REAL FOOD is what your body knows how to process. GMOs, additives, high fructose syrups, to name a few, are foreign to us and guess what? YES! They are stored as fat. You may think you are tricking your body because that food label says fat-free, but what do the ingredients say? That's what your body is reading.

Clean eating is watching your portion sizes and being mindful. We will teach you how to read food labels and educate you on why clean food is the way to go.

This way of eating will not only help you lose weight but will also help reverse the cellular damage caused by yo-yo dieting and years of consuming processed foods, ultimately preventing disease and inflammation in your body.

SNAPSHOT: The Clean Cut Way of Life

- Nothing Processed
- NON-GMO
- Organic, When Possible
- Limiting Sugar
- Healthy Fats
- Portion Control
- Mindfulness
- Foods That Satisfy
- Cheat Meals
- Treats
- Movement
- Proper Hydration
- All-Natural Tricks and Tips
- Proper Sleep
- Mindful Eating

At Clean Cut, we emphasize quality over quantity. It's not a diet, it's a lifestyle! Eating clean is a choice—a decision to replace processed foods with the healthiest and most nutritious ones (most of the time).

The key to success is being prepared. Having a plan makes it easier to stay on track. Prepping your "go-to" foods so that you can grab and go, planning your menu for the week, making extras (equals less time in the kitchen), and making NO EXCUSES means you are a member of the Clean Cut Tribe! We also want you to be realistic. Never say never. This helps keep the balance. We are human, and we will fall. It's not about the falls, it's about how we get back up.

> GO-TO FOOD: Your safe food. A snack or a meal that you know works in your body at specific times of the day or in certain situations. It can always be trusted and is easy to grab.

The Program

Small pivots lead to big changes. Pick one or two things to really focus on (not just food, also your mindset) and work on them until they become part of the new you. Then pick another one to two and continue to make these pivots. Before you know it, you are making real change. Every time you make a food choice, it will be mindful. This type of practice may lead into other parts of your life. When you are kind to yourself with the food you choose, you will find it easier to be kind to yourself in other facets of

> TREAT: In the Clean Cut world, something you like that is outside of the Clean Cut guidelines. It is also something you should enjoy and balance out. For example, a slice of pizza or an extra glass of wine, a few pretzels or some chocolate. These will never sabotage your efforts, but don't let them be a gateway back to old habits.

your life. When you feel clear and focused, you will find you are a better mother, father, friend, son, employee, etc. Perhaps you will exercise and socialize more, or even treat yourself to a massage. Clean Cut is real life, not just food.

> **CHEAT:** A full-blown cheat should also be enjoyed but planned around. What will you do before and after? For example, a full night out including wine, bread, a full meal, and dessert. One cheat isn't the beginning of the end, it's real life, and necessary.

All the fad diets and gimmicks on the market just confuse our body's metabolism, cells and insulin levels. We've caused a traffic jam in our body systems and need to clear them out so our bodies do what they were built for. At the end of the program (also known as the start of your new lifestyle) you will look back at the past decisions you thought were clean, fine, ok, whatever you called them and realize how off you were and how easy it is to make real change. This awareness and understanding is one of the main goals of our program. We will give you the science behind the why helping you to make choices for all the right reasons, not just to fit into your jeans. When eating clean for life you will notice a shift in your energy level, clearer skin, weight loss, stronger nails and hair, better sleep and overall better mental health. Sounds pretty amazing, right? It's simple, and Clean Cut will guide you through it. It is a new lifestyle and while there will be special occasions or "cheat meals," you will be making better food choices and overall, become more mindful in daily life.

How Clean Cut Works

Call it a challenge, mind switch, life change—whatever it is to you, we hope you learn a new way of thinking, living, and thriving. Our goal through this challenge and beyond is to have you think a little differently about your overall health and life habits. Throughout the six weeks, you will learn new eating habits (what to eat; when to eat; portion control), understand calories in versus out, and, nutrient-dense foods and the evils of sugars! You will have a grip on what works in your body, and in your life. You will lose weight, gain muscle, and feel great. Mindful eating and controlling what you put in your body will be your new norm.

We look forward to taking this journey with you.

In this program, you will be supplied:

- Week 1 detox
- A list of foods that are allowed and ones to avoid
- Weekly menu guides and grocery lists
- A variety of recipes throughout the weeks to help you stay satisfied
- Tips on when and what to eat
- Plateau busters
- Natural remedies to assist with sleep, digestion, water retention, and more
- A change in your workout routine to challenge your body in new ways (consistency—not "if I get to the gym," but "when I get to the gym") along with many other fun facts to help you live a healthier life
- A "how to get through social events" guide
- Measurement chart/weigh-in chart
- Access to our private Facebook Clean Cut Book Club
- Weekly goal sheet
- Educational component—i.e. Learn how to read food labels, GMO, etc.

For six weeks you will follow each chapter specifically. By the end, you will have all the tools to complete your new lifestyle.

Measurements and Weight Tracking

There are a lot of ways to track your weight loss progress. The classic scale can be an angel one day and a devil the next. We are not suggesting you forego the bathroom scale, but we would like you to open your mind and see the big picture. There are other essential tools out there for you to track your progress. Our favorite is your inches lost. When losing body fat, you will see inches drop. Sometimes the scale will not move as you might like, but then, BAM! You check your inches and can't believe it! They're down and suddenly, your mindset changes.

You CAN do this!

It IS working!

So, opening your mind to look at your inches lost is a great tool to see your results.

One more way to track your progress is to look at how your clothes fit. To us, this is the most rewarding tracker! Is your belt loop closing in? Are your jeans saggy? What about that tank top you have been dying to look great in?

CLEAN CUT TIP

Find a pair of jeans, a bathing suit, or tank top you want to fit into. Try on that piece of clothing, and remember how it feels. Maybe take a picture. This will be the last time you feel that way in that piece of clothing. Use it as a measurement tool when you track your inches lost. Try it on every three weeks and watch how you change! Besides checking the scale, this is a great way to stay on track and moving toward your goal.

Your measurement chart below is also available online exclusively for you at www.cleancutfit.com/bookclub.

Measurement Circumference Chart

Take your measurements at the beginning of week 1, at the end of week 3 and the end of week 6.

Bust: Place the measuring tape across your nipples (yes we said that) and measure around the largest part of your chest. Be sure to keep the tape parallel to the floor.

Waist: Place the measuring tape about half an inch above your belly button (at the narrowest part of your waist, because who wouldn't want to put it there?) to measure around your torso. When measuring your waist, exhale and measure before inhaling again.

Navel: Isn't that a strange word? Place the measuring tape directly across your naval and measure around your torso.

Hips: OK so for this one you do need to place the measuring tape across the widest part of your hips/buttocks (sorry), and measure all the way around while keeping the tape parallel to the floor.

Thigh: Place the measuring tape on the fullest part (this just sounds nicer than largest) of your thigh and wrap completely around to the starting point.

Upper arm: Place the measuring tape in the center of your upper arm (yes, the bat wing) Wrap the tape measure around the widest part of your upper arm from front to back and around to the start point.

Area	Week 1	End of week 3	End of week 6
DATE			
Bust			
Waist			
Navel			
Hips			
Thigh			
Upper Arm			

Weight Tracking Chart

To calculate percent of weight loss:

Original Weight Minus Your New Weight

Divided by Your Original Weight

(Original Weight – New Weight = Weight Lost)

Original Weight

Date							
Weight							
Percent							

Week 1 NOTES:

_____

_____

_____

_____

Week 2 NOTES:

_____

_____

_____

_____

Week 3 NOTES:

_____

_____

_____

_____

Week 4 NOTES:

_____

_____

_____

_____

Week 5 NOTES:

_____

_____

_____

_____

Week 6 NOTES:

_____

_____

_____

_____

Final NOTES:

_____

_____

_____

_____

_____

All Rules, No Excuses (Play Like a Champion!)

- **Portion size**: For protein, a portion is the size and thickness of your palm (four ounces). For vegetables, pile 'em high—unlimited!

- **Eat slowly**: Put your fork down between bites. Cut each bite at a time. Look at your food, notice the colors, realize it's your energy. Let your body register the food you have consumed.

- **Plate your food:** Look at what you are eating. Pause for a moment and realize how kind you are being to yourself with a colorful plate of clean food.

- **Healthy grabs on the counter:** Because sometimes you just can't wait one more second before you eat. Have healthy foods ready to go on the counter. Nuts, cherry tomatoes, etc.

- **Drink about half of your body weight in ounces of water:** (adding Pink Himalayan helps hydrate, see natural remedies) It may seem like a daunting task but it's always been 8 -8 ounce glasses of water daily. This is one fact that has never changed.

- **Stay away from marinades and cooking sauces with sugar.**

- **Keep sodium low:** Healthy adults should limit to 2,300mg a day or lower. Replace all salts with Pink Himalayan salt and you won't have to think about it.

- **Unlimited unsweetened teas allowed.**

- **Keep snacks in your car** and on-the-go readily available.

- **The dreaded journal:** Whether you like pen and paper or an app, find the tool that works for you. It's key to keeping you on track. In the beginning, journaling is a great tool to help you understand portions and see when you need to get back on track. We love MyFitnessPal.

- **Workouts**: Fitting in those workouts may sometimes be tough but scheduling them like an appointment and getting them done is going to be crucial to your success. You can't out-exercise a bad diet, and no one has ever regretted a finished workout. #nevermissamonday

Blending fitness and nutrition is the answer to long term success.

» More muscle = increased burning of body fat and increased bone density.

» Stronger bone density

» Working out helps stimulate metabolism and endorphins.

» Running three miles = about 300 calories burned. Does that earn you French fries? (CHOICES)

● **Time management:** Managing your clean eating lifestyle is vital. So, follow the preparation rules, schedule those workouts, drink that water, and get some sleep. Weight loss will follow. A time management schedule is at the end of the book.

CLEAN CUT TIP

Your biggest problem will be the excuses you find. Picture where you want to be and work toward it every day.

Chapter 3

Preparing and Planning

Remodeling Your Mindset

Mindset: Clean the slate, throw out everything you think you know about food, grab a drink, and listen up!

Remodeling Your Pantry

You are currently food shopping and cooking now, but your path around the supermarket will change and what is in your cart will change. Your time spent in the kitchen will become more efficient. Here is where you will create your snapshot of the week which will help you stay focused and on track. Preparing and planning your meals is going to be your key to success. Lack of preparation will set you up to fail. This prep doesn't have to be hours of slaving in the kitchen. In this chapter, you will learn the secrets and tools for the Clean Cut way of prepping.

Why is prep so important? We all have busy lives. Taking some time to plan and prep your meals will take the guesswork out of what to eat and when. You won't be stuck at a baseball game or swim practice staring at a vending machine, trying to make a "healthy choice." Once you get into a rhythm, preparing will just become part of your daily routine.

Your Step by Step Prep Guide

Preparing begins with organizing your week:

1. What does your schedule look like?
   - Weekly social events?
   - Late nights with kids' activities?
   - Work?
   - Commute?

2. Make sure you have proper storage containers for your snacks and meals, and if you need to bring those meals to work in a cooler, make sure to have one ready to go. Oh and don't forget your prepped food in the fridge in the morning, leave yourself a post-it note until it becomes part of your routine. Purchase a water bottle you will actually use. Caren likes one with a straw and Lori likes to have a handle on hers. Go with whatever you like. As long as you are drinking water, we are smiling!

3. Look over your menu guides and choose your recipes for the week. Now, check off what you need on your grocery list, decide what your staples will be (Go-To Grabs) and hit the supermarket.

4. Prepare your Go-To Grabs. "What's a Go-to Grab?" you ask. It's what works for you in your lifestyle. These are the safe, easy foods that work for you on the go. They can also be a staple meal in your house that works for you and your family. These are the foods that are always in your refrigerator and are ready to grab when needed. They travel easily and keep

you satisfied. Your Go-To Grabs might be different than ours, and they might change week by week. Regardless, they are prepared and ready when needed:

- Hard-boiled eggs
- Egg cups (see recipes)
- Nuts
- Chicken and tuna salads (YUP, with real mayo! More to come in Chapter 6)
- Avocado

5. Make for dinner, have for lunch. While already in the kitchen, this is where you save time and cook extra to use later. You will notice some of our recipes and guides are designed to include portions for dinner with enough left over to have for lunch the next day.

6. Portion out your snacks. For example, make small snack baggies of 1 ounce about 10 almonds for each day of the week. Grab and go with your green apple. Look at that, 1 snack done! Easy stuff!

Cut up your veggies, and have them ready to just grab and go from the refrigerator.

CLEAN CUT TIP

Time Saver Tip! You can buy pre-packaged single-serving nuts and veggies. Supermarkets make it so easy these days. Nuts are portioned, and veggies are spiralized, cut, and riced for you!

Visit our website for up-to-date great finds to make it easy to stay on track: www.cleancutfit.com.

CHAPTER 4

The Education and the Why

(This is very important and will help you pause

and think before you take your next bite.)

Meet your Good Fats

Learning to trust good fat can be a challenge. Good fat is your friend and sugar is your enemy. Your body understands real food. Trying to trick the body with processed options only causes it to store fat while simultaneously creating inflammation and increasing your chances for disease. Good fat not only burns fat (we'll explain below) but also keeps you full and satisfied. It also limits your insulin spikes. The days of sugar-free, fat-free, and yo-yo dieting fads could have been the cause of your weight gain. Those diets wreak havoc by causing your body to release too much insulin, too often leaving your body no chance to use it. Instead, high blood insulin levels cause excess sugar in the blood to be stored as FAT. At Clean Cut, we believe that your main source of energy should be from good dietary fats and your STORED body fat. Sounds kind of fun, right?

What are good fats?

MCT (medium chain triglycerides):

Olive Oil

Avocado Oil

Coconut Oil

Raw Coconut

Nut butters

Nuts of any kind

Avocado

Eggs

Irish butter or Ghee

Fat from protein

These types of fats contain fat-soluble nutrients needed for health. Without them, we cannot absorb the amount we need for true health. Our brain is made up of 60% fat so why wouldn't we feed it what it wants to gain more mental clarity? Our cell walls are also made up of fat, and again, without eating the good ones, our hormones cannot pass through the cell walls to do what they are meant to do. If the hormones cannot pass through, it leads to weight gain and low energy. When faced with a hormone imbalance, all systems will not work properly. Imagine feeling energized and winning the fight against aging just by adding in these good fats and removing the enemy— sugar. When you begin to trust that good fats are the primary source of our energy and add in the correct amount, you will begin to use stored fat as additional energy. That will ultimately help you break through the roadblock to become the new you. It's all about... BALANCE!!!

Is there such a thing as eating too much good fat? What is the correct balance of daily good fats? Like anything in life, we need moderation and balance.

The dietary reference intake (DRI) for fat in adults is 20 to 35 percent of total calories from fat. An adult female consuming roughly 1,500 to 2,000 calories daily, should consume 44 to 77 grams of good fats daily to maintain a healthy, balanced diet. (20 to 35 percent equals 400 to 700 calories. Dividing those numbers by nine calories per gram results in an ideal consumption of roughly 44 to 77 grams of fat per day.) For a physically active man, for example, 3,000 calories is a nice number, which translates to roughly 66 to 116 grams of fat.

Eating the correct amount of healthy fat daily will help your body burn fat. However, like anything else, if you eat too much of a good thing, you will gain weight instead.

We are teaching you to find the balance and what works for you to lose weight, manage it, LIVE, fight disease and find a new level of energy and freedom.

Here is a list of the good fats we recommend along with their serving sizes and grams of fat per each:

One full medium avocado = 22 grams of fat

One handful of nuts = 13 grams of fat

One full egg = 4.5 grams of fat

One tablespoon of olive or coconut oil = 14 grams of fat

One tablespoon of Irish butter = 12 grams of fat

One tablespoon of a nut butter = 9 grams of fat

Now let's put this all together in the CLEAN CUT lifestyle:

If you have two to three full eggs a day, one full medium-sized avocado, half a serving of nuts (half a handful), half a serving of a nut butter (that would be 1½ teaspoons), one tablespoon of Irish butter and one teaspoon of an oil, you will have consumed 73 grams of good fat, which is perfect. Remember some days will be less and some more. It's all a balance. So, next time you are thinking about your days and weeks as a whole, try to find the balance in your fats. Seventy-three grams a day should be keeping you plenty full and satisfied, all while helping you burn fat.

*Healthy eating.com
*ClevelandClinic.org

Insulin

Insulin is a hormone produced by your pancreas. It helps your body metabolize carbohydrates, fats, and proteins and turns glucose (sugar in your bloodstream from your food) into energy. It unlocks cells so the glucose can enter them and be converted to energy or stored for later use. (And without the good fat, it's harder to break into these cells). The glucose cannot be used as energy unless it's inside your cells, liver or muscles. Without insulin, glucose will just float around in your bloodstream and build up. When glucose builds up in your bloodstream, your blood sugar levels rise. If this goes on for a long period of time, it causes damage in so many ways. Your body will lose the ability to send the correct messages to your brain, and in turn, send out more insulin, damaging your organs, nerves, and blood vessels. If you are constantly asking your body for more insulin with your dietary choices (high carbohydrate or sugar meals) or the frequency of eating, you are not only breaking down your system, you are sending the message to store fat. And, your body will not tap into the already stored energy (glucose or fat), causing weight gain or even worse, diabetes.

*www.healthline.com

Eating the Clean Cut way is designed for your life...a real, HEALTHY life.

When you eat the correct foods at the correct time with the correct portions, you will find yourself with more energy because you are breaking down stored energy and fat simply from keeping your insulin hormone levels low. The fewer highs and lows you have with insulin, the more efficient your metabolism will be due to the correct usage of this system.

How can we make sure we don't become insulin resistant (the inability to use insulin correctly) and help manage our health?

Any food with fast-burning carbs (bagels, pasta, added sugars, processed, etc.) acts like flint to fire and burns up quickly, leaving you hungry. So, you eat again, asking your pancreas for even more insulin to help push the excess blood glucose into your cells. Our goal is to help you find the foods that keep you satisfied, so that urge to graze goes away. Mindless grazing is a big factor in weight gain due to excess calorie consumption and slowing the metabolism. Grazing causes sustained elevated sugars in your blood which means your body is releasing more insulin to help absorb it into your cells. We want our bodies to use the already stored glucose and fat as energy not a constant stream of it. When we have this constant stream our bodies have one choice but to store it as fat.

That is why we urge you to focus on GOOD FATS. Not only do they turn on your fat burning system, but they also keep you full, and have a low insulin spike. It's nice to give your body a break from digestion and not feel hungry every three hours.

Safe Foods with Health Benefits and Low Glycemic Index (Low Insulin)

These top ten foods are in no particular order. They all have such a low glycemic value that your body doesn't need much insulin to absorb them. Our goal is to keep that insulin level down, so your metabolism is constantly working.

The foods you choose should have a slow digestion and absorption rate. Our goal is to keep our insulin levels low and steady. Living a lifestyle like this will lead to overall better health and weight loss.

Natural fruits, veggies, proteins, and fats all break down more slowly keeping insulin levels low.

1. Onion and Garlic (full of vitamins and anti-inflammatory benefits)
2. Leafy Greens (our Superfoods)
3. Nuts (anti-inflammatory, good fats, low carb, high fiber)
4. Seeds (Pumpkin, sunflower, and chia seeds are great to use instead of granolas. Use on salads for added fiber, good fats, and nutrients.)
5. Avocados (omega 3 and 6 fatty acids and amazing nutrients)
6. Coconut (any form, oil, meat, flakes, flour, it's the perfect fat)
7. Herbs (full of flavor, minerals, vitamins, some healing properties)
8. Eggs (vitamin B12, protein, and fat; cheap and easy)
9. Irish Butter and Cheese (Eat cheese in moderation. Dairy causes the body to become acidic and inflamed. Make sure it has no growth hormones in it.)

10. Oils (organic is best: olive, coconut, avocado. Stay away from palm oil, canola.)

When cooking or snacking, add any of these to guarantee a low insulin level.

*YouTube: Eric Berg DC, Glycemic Index vs. Insulin

Emotional Eating: Why We Need to PAUSE

Whether it's a major situation or daily stresses in life, we are all triggered by emotions and typically they will appear in our eating habits. Everyone has a relationship with food. What is yours?

What you will learn in this book is that most of your eating habits are just that—habits. They are the constant cause and effect of what you've always done and continue to do. We are here to let you know that breaking habits is possible, even the nasty emotional eating ones. We will guide you through it with all our steps to a healthy Clean Cut YOU!!

Any emotional situation that drives you to overeat will always end in the same result. After the high of the eating or the rush of the sugar, the emotions return and then you are typically left with a new emotion called guilt!! And the cycle continues...your emotions trigger you to overeat, you beat yourself up for getting off your weight-loss track, you feel bad, and you eat again. Around and around we go, back into old habits.

Sometimes the strongest food cravings hit when you're at your weakest point emotionally. You may turn to food for comfort. This may happen consciously or unconsciously. When we're faced with a difficult problem, feeling stressed or even feeling bored, angry or happy, food becomes a comfort.

Food can help suppress or soothe emotions like stress, anger, fear, boredom, fatigue, sadness and loneliness. Any of these intense feelings can lead to emotional eating and disrupt your weight-loss efforts. It's a fact that your emotions can become so tied to your eating habits that whenever you're angry or stressed you will automatically reach for a treat without thinking about it. If it happens every once in a while, it's easy to undo. If you let it become an excuse, it will always be your roadblock.

Although some people eat less when faced with strong emotions. Others who are in an emotional state might turn to impulsive or even binge eating, quickly consuming whatever's convenient or off limits without enjoyment. Unfortunately, they are also typically comfort-type foods, which are higher in sugar and calories.

Mantras

To truly be successful in any part of life it's necessary to PAUSE. Take a minute and look at the situation ahead of you, whether it's with food, work, family, friends or shopping. If you pause, you will most likely make a better choice.

> MANTRA: A slogan, saying or positive word you can repeat or look at to keep you in check, helping you to pause and think before you make a choice.

Clean Cut mantras are a great tool to give you that pause, and they allow you to decide with a clear head. Ask yourself these questions:

- How do I want to feel tomorrow?
- What do I need to do today?
- Is it worth it?

- How will I feel after?
- Do I want to give back all my hard work for this?
- Should I save it for my cheat?
- Am I really still hungry?

Pause and evaluate before making the decision.

CHOICES: Worth Repeating Because They're THAT Important

It's all about choices. Fruit or wine? Grazing or committing? Mindless eating or mindfulness? It really comes down to not making up excuses and staying focused. All our foods in this Clean Cut program, all the tips and tools help keep you satisfied and mindful. When you put them to use you will be amazed that, more often than not, you can pause and make the right choice.

Your Schedule: Prep Your Mind

Life happens. We have busy lives with jobs, kids, and commitments. But you've already decided to make this lifestyle change by preparing and planning. Let's take a step in "growing your mind." For example, we know that after we drop the kids off, we head to teach a class, get a workout in or work on our online business.

We are aware and ready for our day. We know what's happening. We may be intermittent fasting or have snacks with us. Meeting for lunch? We know where we are going and know the CHOICES there. When we pick up the kids at the end of the day, it may be time for afternoon snack. Always being prepared and figuring out your go-to foods, whether on the road or at home, becomes part of your lifestyle. Figuring out those trusted "GO-TO" meals or grabs is key to success. Having a plan will prevent you from staring at the refrigerator and craving something just because you are bored. Write it out and schedule time for the important things in your life. Block them out on your calendar. Some examples are:

- Prep
- Work
- Free Time/Family/Friends
- Self-Care (workout, massage, personal appointments)
- Administration
- Meals
- Commute
- Personal Development

Do you get the picture? Scheduling a workout is like scheduling a doctor's appointment. If you needed a doctor, would you blow it off? Is your body in need of a healthy lifestyle? Don't blow it off. Scheduling and planning are going to be part of your tools in your Clean Cut Toolbox.

Natural Remedies: Tools to Keep Your Gut Healthy, Stay Hydrated, and Reset Your System

The Clean Cut way leads you to real foods. A natural progression would be to look at the earth's remedies and keep it real! Some of our top natural remedies include apple cider vinegar, Himalayan Pink Salt, and a good probiotic. **Without a healthy gut, you are fighting a losing battle. We need to get your gut clean first to make all the other systems work together.**

Apple Cider Vinegar

The high content of acetic acid (the GOOD BACTERIA) added to the two-part fermenting process makes this vinegar healthy for your gut. Most health and weight issues start with poor gut health so:

Probiotics + Apple Cider Vinegar = Healthy Gut, Healthy You

We recommend organic unfiltered brands because they contain the "mother." This is the stuff that settles to the bottom— the good stuff. It contains the strands of protein, enzymes and that good bacteria.

Real Science:

In one study, the participants that reduced their calorie intake by 250 calories and added in a total of two tablespoons of Apple Cider Vinegar lost an average of 8.8 pounds over 12 weeks. The participants who did not receive ACV only lost 5 pounds over the 12-week study period. The researchers also found that ACV decreased cholesterol levels.

Uchicagomedicine.org (Written by Edwin McDonald IV, MD)

Apple Cider Vinegar slows down the emptying of your stomach, creating the feeling of fullness, while initially lowering the blood sugar levels right after a higher carbohydrate meal (again making you feel full, so you are eating fewer calories daily).

The vinegar also contains an antioxidant called chlorogenic acid which protects your LDL cholesterol levels. YAY! This is what studies show decreases cholesterol levels. Because apple cider vinegar lowers your blood sugar (glucose) and insulin when taken before a higher carbohydrate meal, it will actually lower LDL levels as well. This sounds like a natural miracle to us!!

Proven Benefits of Acetic Acid (The main difference between apple cider vinegar and other kinds of vinegar.)

- Helps lower blood sugar levels after a higher carbohydrate meal

- Decreases insulin levels, improves insulin sensitivity, helps to ensure your body keeps sending the correct messages to the brain

- Reduces fat storage by activating your metabolism causing your system to use stored fat as fuel instead of storing more fat

- Suppresses appetite by promoting a fullness because it delays stomach emptying

*Healthline.com (Written by Kris Gunnars BSC)

How to Use It:

The recommended dose for these health benefits is 1–2 table-spoons (15–30 ml) per day, mixed with water. You can also add it to food like salad dressing or cook with it. It's easier to drink when it's cold so leave it in the refrigerator.

It seems to make sense to have it before meals since it will help promote fullness and is in your system ready to take on your food. Taking it a half hour or so before is best but any time you can get it in will still have health benefits. Taking more than the recommended dose can be potentially harmful by lowering your blood potassium and creating bone loss.

Start with 1 teaspoon (5 ml) to see how you tolerate it. Do not take more than 1 tablespoon at a time add to the end make you feel nauseous at first. Once you know how you feel on it then you can start to add more, never more the 2 tablespoons daily.

It's a cheap, simple way, when used properly, to guard you from illness, disease, and weight gain. So, give it a try!

*Healthline.com (Medically reviewed by Debra Rosa Wilson, PhD, MSN, RN, IBCLC, AHN-BC, CHT)

Pink Himalayan salt. Are You Dehydrated?

How can you be? You drink half your body weight in ounces of water, right?

Some classic signs of dehydration are:

- Dry mouth
- Dull headache
- Muscle cramps
- Heart palpitations
- Lightheadedness
- Weakness
- Decrease in urine output or it's dark yellow in color

Do you have any of these?

We've been told that water makes up approximately 45–75% of our body weight. We want to absorb this water into our cells (known as intracellular). When we can't absorb it correctly the water stays on the outside of our cells (known as extracellular). This is when we retain water (think swollen fingers and feet). Water is an essential nutrient that we cannot live without it.

Here's a fun fact: There are three ways we lose water; sweating, elimination (urination and bowel movements), and breathing—yes, breathing. You know that smoke you see coming out of your mouth when it's cold out? Yup, it's water. The combination of all three is approximately 2.2 liters of water a day (2.0 liters a day from sweating and elimination and 0.2 from breathing). Now you know why you've always been told to drink eight cups of water a day. Eight cups = your 2.2 liters (roughly 68 ounces). Note: if you add exercise into your daily routine, your water intake must also increase.

So how can we ensure all the fluids we are drinking are being absorbed into our cells keeping us hydrated and supporting our overall cellular health?

The solution: Himalayan Pink Salt. This really is the salt of the earth. It's the salt that does the trick.

Here's a little history on this essential nutrient:

Himalayan Pink Salt is mined in the Himalayan Mountains from an ancient sea bed (approximately 250,000 million years old) which maintains its purity. You may ask, "Why not sea salt?" For example, Celtic Sea Salt? Well, as we all know, the oceans are contaminated. Hence, so is sea salt.

Here's how this amazing natural product works. Himalayan Pink Salt is very different from table salt. Table salt has been stripped of all its nutrients and minerals leaving it with just one, *sodium chloride*, which will not absorb into your cells. Himalayan Pink Salt has 84 trace minerals needed to keep our bodies regulated and working properly.

First, we'll tell you how to use it in your daily life then we'll list all the amazing benefits of this mineral from the earth.

STOP using any other salt ever, ever again. Replace it with Himalayan Pink Salt.

According to Dr. Carolyn Dean, adding ⅛–¼ teaspoon to every liter of water you drink has enormous health benefits. You can cook with it, top your food with it or even just eat it straight up. I can promise—you will NOT retain water using any of these methods. Additionally, forget all the sports drinks, most of them contain nothing but sugar or a sugar substitute.

The health benefits match some of those with magnesium. Imagine how simple it is to put these two in your life, and how much better you will feel.

The benefits of Himalayan Pink Salt:

1. Improves hydration, giving your body 84 minerals it needs to allow your cells to absorb water

2. Balances PH levels bringing them to a more alkaline level (healthy zone)

3. Balances blood sugar levels (works with your thyroid and adrenal glands and supports hormone balance, which all lead to weight management)

4. Improves vascular health, lowering blood pressure

5. Cleanses the sinuses, post nasal drip, lung function and acts as an antihistamine

6. Reduces risk and aids in asthma

7. Increases absorption in your gut and helps detox the digestive tract

8. Calms inflammation of the skin, like an eczema

9. Helps reduce the signs of aging by hydrating your skin with antioxidant properties

10. Improves your sleeping habits

11. Increases bone strength

12. Reduces muscle cramps and acts as a natural electrolyte

13. Helps the central nervous system communicate, which is the center of it all

14. Oh—and enhances libido :-)

*Dr. Alan Mandell, YouTube channel, @motivationaldoc

Not only is this salt delicious, now you can enjoy it knowing it will hydrate you along with providing all these other amazing health benefits. Another easy, cheap, simple tip to add to your already new healthy lifestyle.

The Scoop about Probiotics

The balance between the good and bad bacteria in your gut is directly related to your physical, mental and emotional moods. Don't believe us? Studies have proven that your gut acts like your second brain. Yup, 80 percent of your immune system is located in your gut. If 80 percent is there, imagine how it can affect the other systems in your body. Think we need to focus on gut nutrition?

The Microflora:

The bacteria in our gut play many roles. Yes, they aid in digestion, but without proper digestion, we don't absorb our vitamins and nutrients correctly which can lead to type 2 diabetes, mood swings, weight gain, arthritis, IBS, and even cancer. Remember we noted that 80 percent of our immune system comes from our gut? So, let's treat it right. Eating sugar and processed foods will only allow the bad bacteria to grow, outnumbering the good flora. When 85 percent of your bacteria is good, and 15% or less is bad, that is a healthy balance. Just another reason to eat clean.

Probiotics:

You've all heard of them. Now let's dig a little deeper to understand what foods have them and how simply adding them to your daily routine can create a consistently healthy gut. Gut health is an ongoing process. You must take care of it every day. Choosing to take a probiotic supplement is a great way to ensure gut health. It must contain at least 20 to 30 billion bacteria in each capsule and you need to take them correctly. Most probiotics are not time released so they should be taken on an empty stomach or before bed. If you take them before a meal, wait 20 minutes before you begin eating.

Another natural way to get probiotics is from the foods we consume, which have 100 times more probiotics than any supplement. Remember, we need to have a continuous source of good bacteria going into our systems to replenish them. This is not a quick fix, it's part of your daily routine! The secret to getting probiotics through your food is fermented foods like:

Tempeh: It's a natural, fermented soybean with a nutty taste and contains all the essential amino acids so it's a perfect source of protein.

Miso paste: It's made from barley, rice, or soybean and has a bold taste so a little goes a long way. Careful, this one is high in sodium.

Sauerkraut: It's cabbage with salt and contains fiber. Yum!

Kimchi: The Spicy Asian version of sauerkraut (but even better) helps boost metabolism because of the spice!

Yogurt: Greek is best but try to get organic. Make sure the label says, "Contains live and active cultures."

Kefir: It's fermented milk like a drinkable yogurt. Note the commercial brands have additives so go all natural or organic with this.

Simple! Let's try it and see. Nothing to lose but weight, mood swings, and digestive issues, right?

*Wyndhamhealth.com by Debbie
Drake.com by Jillian Levy, CHHC
Youtube: Dr. Mercola

Intermittent Fasting

Intermittent fasting is not a diet, but rather a dieting pattern.

In simpler terms—it's making a conscious decision to skip certain meals.

Let's start with breaking the myth that if you skip a meal, you will slow your metabolism. In fact, the opposite is true. We told you to throw out everything you think you know about food. We have become so conditioned to think, low-fat, fat-free, don't skip a meal, blah, blah, blah, when in fact, all the science points us in the other direction. Good fats help you lose fat. Fasting helps you burn fat, and your body knows what to do with real food. This "short cut" or "trick" is one of our favorites because it works, and it's free. BUT WHY DOES IT WORK?

With intermittent fasting, your body operates differently than when "feasting."

We taught you that when you eat a meal, your body releases insulin causing glucose levels to rise in the blood, which then our bodies use as energy, right? This process can take a few hours. During this time, your body is using that food as its source of energy. This is what food is for—energy. This is especially true if you just consumed carbohydrates/sugar. Those fast-burning carbs act like flint to a fire and burn up quickly leaving you feeling hungry, which is why we keep pushing good fats at each meal or snack. (Are you starting to trust us?)

During a fasting state, your body doesn't have a source of readily available fuel for energy. Ok, this is the magic part of our bodies. It will find energy from the next source, and then the next. If we let our bodies rest and not use the constant food consumed, we tap into that stored fat as energy, rather than the glucose from our bloodstream from the food we just consumed.

We LOVE the sound of this and live by it.

The same goes for working out in a fasting state. Without a supply of glucose and glycogen to pull from your bloodstream (from food) your body has no choice but to use fat as it's source of energy. Fasting and working out is a win/win for breaking down stored fat!

There are a few different ways to take advantage of intermittent fasting:

For example, only eating from noon to 8 p.m., essentially skipping breakfast (BREAK-FAST). Some people are hungrier in the morning and will eat from 8 a.m. to 4 or 5 p.m.

Some people fast every other day for 14–16 hours (that is your goal when fasting), or every third day. When you find what works for you, and are consistent, you will see and feel the results. And the best part is, IT'S FREE. If you are starving one day, then don't fast. If you truly aren't hungry another day, hold the fast even longer. If you had a big cheat the day before, fast longer. (You have plenty of stored food from your cheat.)

REMEMBER your give and take. This is a great tool to undo a bad choice or to break through to the next level. It's also a great maintenance tool and gives you more wiggle room in your diet choices.

We challenge you to try it for at least three days throughout the week and see the change. We can promise it works.

*YouTube Channel, Thomas DeLauer,
Everything you need to know a about intermittent Fasting

CHAPTER 5

Are You Ready to Shrink Your Body and Grow Your Mind?

How Does Each Week Look?

Week One: The cleanse—no sugar at all (means no fruit either), no complex carbs at all, real food like lean proteins, veggies, and good fats, but yes, you can still have your coffee (First cup the way you like it. If very light and sweet, try to dial it back a bit and see how it goes.) We promise you won't be hungry, you eat real food and we've created "unlimiteds" so you can Keep Calm & Cleanse.

Week Two: Similar to week one but we add in beans. Because beans make a meal feel more hearty and comforting. These have carbs but also tons of fiber, so they process differently in your body. They also add some depth to your meals. Still no fruit and sugar. Clean cocktails come in!

Week Three: This is the week we introduce complex carbs and some fruit. It's once a day or every other day. It's not every meal, and it never will be. This phase is real life. This is where we want you to end up—the balance. You can have quinoa, sprouted breads, small sweet potatoes, some brown rice, small apples, berries, some mango, etc. It's all about portions and triggers. This is where you will learn a lot about your habits and triggers.

Week Four: Oh week four. This week we really work the program, putting together your first three weeks and finding your real lasting "go-to" foods, the ones you will continue to go back to and enjoy and keep you on track. You will become hyper focused on your triggers and not look for excuses. This is the week we want you to break through those old habits calling you back because it's becoming work and the thrill of something new is wearing off. This is the pivotal week to stay the course to really see what is on the other side.

Week Five: You've trusted and stayed the course now let's talk about the recharge or your plateau busters. Week five can be used to practice intermittent fasting or finding a pattern that works for you to live life and continue to lose or maintain your goal weight. This week we challenge you to maybe do week one for ½ the week then add back in some carbs and fruits or maybe go vegetarian for a few days to shock the body cells and make new change to keep the focus. In truth this lifestyle may take a full 6 months to a year to really fix what is broken from so many years of ups and downs. So stay with it and know in the end you have more wiggle room when all systems are a go!!!!

Week Six: We pull it all together, clear up any lingering challenges you may be facing, and as always, we are right here to support you in your continued journey to REAL LIFE BALANCE. Keep following us on Facebook, Instagram, and our site to keep you accountable. There is always a new challenge around the corner.

What Food Can You Eat?

Here is a list of the foods you are allowed always. More will be added as the weeks go on. If there is something not on the list you are unsure of, here is a rule of thumb, if it's a vegetable you can eat it. If you really only like carrots and snap peas we would rather that than chips and crackers. We cannot list every food you can have, but this is a good base guide for you to follow and more popular clean eats. Always ask questions on the Facebook Book Board. It's better to have asked than to make a mistake.

TOOL BOX TIP

Net carbohydrates are what you're left with after subtracting the grams of fiber per serving from the total carbohydrate amount per serving. For example, if an item has 20 grams of carbohydrates and it contains 8 grams of fiber, then the amount of net carbs, the ones your body reacts to is a total of 12 grams.

Protein: Limit to four ounces per serving.

- Crab
- Chicken
- Shrimp
- Beef (lean)
- Scallops
- Whitefish
- Veal
- Buffalo
- Albacore white tuna
- Salmon

- Scoop of plant-based protein powder (sweetened with Stevia or no sweetener)
- Full eggs and egg whites
- Organic tempeh/organic cold processed/sprouted tofu (Nasoya at Whole Foods)

Good Fats: They won't make you fat. We promise! Good Fats are known as MCT (Medium Chain Triglycerides). These help your metabolism to use fat as fuel.

TIP: Remember, you gain weight from consuming sugar.

- Olive Oil
- Olives
- Avocado Oil
- Avocado
- Walnut Oil
- Walnuts
- Almonds
- Pistachios
- Cashews
- Macadamia Nuts
- Nuts of any kind
- Irish Butter (can find in a grocery store) YES, BUTTER, just not on Italian bread!
- Coconut Oil (MCT)
- Coconut Cubes
- Nut butters (sugar should be less than 2 grams)

Vegetables: Unlimited, GMO-FREE (This is important. Be aware, if corn is not organic, it is most likely GMO. There is new data saying that GMO produce is no longer labeled as such. Researching this... stay tuned. To be safe, go organic if you can.

- Lettuce
- Asparagus
- Spinach
- Tomatoes
- Cucumber
- Cabbage
- Onion
- Radishes
- Fennel
- Celery
- Kale
- Cauliflower
- Peppers
- Zucchini
- Root Veggies
- Swiss Chard
- Broccoli
- Really any and all veggies
- GMO-FREE!

Spices:

Spices are amazing flavor booster, so have at it!! Any spices are great! Our favorites are garlic, ginger, pepper and Pink Himalayan salt. Pink Himalayan salt (not sea salt) doesn't act like high sodium foods in our bodies so if you are a salt lover go ahead and enjoy. Salts are known to help burn fat because of the minerals.

CLEAN CUT TIP

Have questions about something not on this list? Post your question in the Facebook Clean Cut Book Club board.

Ready to shrink your body and grow your mind? Here we go!

CHAPTER 6

Your "Detox" Week

Week 1

This program is designed to turn on your fat burning system and shut down your fat storing one. All the foods we choose and put together will do just that. Getting your body to work as it should takes time. So, be patient. All the years of fat-free, sugar-free, yo-yo diets, processed foods, chemicals, and stress causes our metabolism to slow down. We want to help you reverse that. Over the next six weeks, we will educate you on how. The key is CONSISTENCY! Without it, the results you are looking for will be harder to reach.

Setting Your Goals

This program is all about YOU. Be selfish and really think about why you took this step. Everyone is different and has different goals. Looking at these goals throughout your journey will help you through cravings and keep you focused. Each week you will be asked a set of questions about your experience. Journaling these thoughts is a great way to look back and see what worked, and find your balance. These questions can also be found in PDF format on your book club page.

What are your goals?

Why do you want to be healthy and fit?

Who will be supporting you through this adventure?

Short-term goals (1 month and 3 months):

Long-term goals (6 months to 1 year or more):

What are your top "challenges?" (This could be too much soda, sugar, no time to prep meals, portion sizes, etc.)

What You May NOT Eat Week 1

- Sugar of any kind. This includes but is not limited to cake, cookies, white bread,
- pastas, and processed foods.
- Dairy (for now; we will add it back in later)
- Complex carbohydrates (like grains)

CLEAN CUT TIP

In week 1, there is a detox veggie soup recipe. This soup is unlimited with just the veggies in it. It is a great way to curb a hunger craving, especially as you are detoxing from sugar. You can have it chunky or puree it for a smooth consistency.

Coconut wraps are a great alternative to a flour-based wrap! Great healthy fats and low calorie, these are a winner!

Remember you are now eating to live, not living to eat.

Week 1 Menu Guide

Day 1		
Breakfast	**Lunch**	**Dinner**
3 eggs: 1–2 full eggs and 1 white loaded with veggies (use olive oil or real Irish butter in the pan) with ½ an avocado **OR** 2 hard-boiled eggs with ½ an avocado	Fresh salad with 4 ounces chicken breast or ½ cup of Chicken/Tuna Salad (see recipes) over a salad **OR** 4 ounces turkey breast (about 4–5 slices; nitrate-free) with half an avocado (this is your fat)	Slow Cooker Shredded Chicken and Salsa (see recipes) with any veggies as a side (see veggie recipes)
Snack	**Snack**	**Snack**
10 nuts	Veggies ¼ cup hummus	Veggie Detox Soup

Day 2		
Breakfast	**Lunch**	**Dinner**
EGGvocado (see recipes) **OR** Eggs any way with ½ an avocado or 2 egg cups (should be prepped)	Leftover shredded chicken with ½ avocado and tomato (cherry or sliced) **OR** ½ cup tuna or chicken salad with big salad	Eggroll in a Bowl (see recipes)
Snack	**Snack**	**Snack**
3 turkey roll-ups with roasted red pepper and a few slices of avocado	Veggie Detox Soup	1 tablespoon nut butter

Day 3		
Breakfast	**Lunch**	**Dinner**
Clean Cut Eggvocado (see recipes) **OR** 2 egg cups If you don't want eggs, have tuna or chicken salad with ½ an avocado or 2 slices of bacon.	Leftover Egg Roll in a Bowl **OR** ½ cup tuna or chicken salad with big salad	Shrimp and Peppers (see recipes) **OR** 6 ounces grilled fish Over Cauliflower Rice side (see recipes)
Snack	**Snack**	**Snack**
10 nuts	Grilled chicken strips dipped in hot sauce or mustard **OR** 2 hard-boiled eggs	¼ cup hummus with veggies (Try something different like fennel!)

Day 4

Breakfast	Lunch	Dinner
Green Juice (see recipes)	Leftover shrimp, if any, over a big salad with vinaigrette (see recipes) **OR** Any other lunch options like ½ cup tuna wrapped in a turmeric coconut wrap (can be found in any health store)	Pesto Turkey or Chicken Meatball with Roasted String Beans side (see recipes) or Brussels sprouts (see recipes)
Snack	**Snack**	**Snack**
Veggie Detox Soup	Veggies with ¼ cup hummus **OR** 2 hard-boiled eggs **OR** Leftover chicken, if still some left	Chicken breast strips dipped in honey mustard **OR** 2 pesto meatballs **OR** 1 tablespoon nut butter

Day 5		
Breakfast	**Lunch**	**Dinner**
1 serving Sun-Dried Tomato Quiche (see recipes)	Protein over a big salad with homemade vinaigrette and ½ avocado Some examples: 4 ounces turkey lunch meat, tuna or chicken salad, leftover turkey meatballs	Turkey Taco Stuffed Peppers (see recipes)
Snack	**Snack**	**Snack**
Raw nuts (10)	Chopped veggies ¼ cup hummus	2 hard-boiled eggs

Day 6

Breakfast	Lunch	Dinner
1 serving sun-Dried Tomato Quiche (left over)	Leftover stuffed peppers **OR** Slice of quiche with ½ avocado and side salad and cup of detox soup **OR** Tuna/chicken salad with veggies or big salad and 1 cup detox soup	Butternut squash sauce on any protein with a side of veggie of choice
Snack	**Snack**	**Snack**
4 slices of turkey rolled with roasted peppers and a slice of avocado	10 nuts	1 tablespoon nut butter

Day 7

Breakfast	Lunch	Dinner
Green Juice (see recipes) **OR** Eggs any way	Leftovers from dinner or your go-to lunch that has been working for you	Cauliflower Rice (see recipes)
Snack	**Snack**	**Snack**
Cup of detox soup with scoop of tuna/chicken/turkey roll-up	Turkey roll-ups with hummus **OR** The snack that has been working for you	1 tablespoon nut butter

Week 1 Recipes

Clean Cut Detoxing Vegetable Soup*

- 1 onion diced
- 2 carrots chopped
- 3 celery stalks chopped
- ½ to 1 zucchini, chopped (depending on size)
- 3 garlic cloves, chopped
- 1 can organic diced tomatoes (or FRESH!)
- 32 ounces low-sodium broth of your choice (chicken, vegetable or miso)
- 1 tablespoon fresh rosemary
- 1 tablespoon fresh thyme
- 2 handfuls of chopped kale and/or spinach
- 1 teaspoon fresh lemon juice
- Salt and pepper to taste
- Water

Heat large stockpot and add 1 tablespoon coconut or olive oil, sauté onion, carrots, zucchini and celery. Cook until tender, about 5 minutes. Add in garlic and cook for 2–3 minutes more.

Pour in your broth and tomatoes. Add seasonings. Cook for 10–15 minutes more. Stir in your greens and add lemon juice. Add water to get desired consistency (depending if you want more of a stew, or thinner soup). Salt and pepper to taste. Warm and enjoy! *You can add any type of veggies you want for this soup.

One bowl is a serving, but you can have this unlimited through your program.

Per serving: 65 Calories; 0 g Fat; 3.5 g Protein; 13 g Carbohydrate; 4 g Fiber; 5g Sugar

Egg Cups

- 1 dozen eggs 6 full (this is your fat) 6 white
- Chopped veggies of choice, peppers, onion, asparagus, spinach, etc.

Muffin tin sprayed with natural spray. You can use a 6-muffin pan or a 12-cupcake pan.

Heat oven to 350° F.

Stuff each cup with a blend of the veggies to the top.

Whisk the eggs and pour over each cup to just below the rim.

Bake for 18–20 minutes. In the last few minutes, add a slice of tomato to each to roast.

Let cool slightly on wire rack and place in a fridge-safe container. Pop two in the microwave for 30 seconds to one minute, depending on your microwave, for a simple breakfast or snack.

Options: Use salsa in each or on top or use nitrate-free cold cuts and place on the bottom of each cup then add veggies.

If using a 6-muffin tin, 1 muffin is a serving. If using a 12-cupcake tin, 2 cupcakes are a serving.

Per Serving: 156 Calories; 17 g Protein; 4 g Carbohydrate; 1.3 g Fiber; 2 g Sugar; 7 g Fat

The Perfect Hard-Boiled Egg:

Bring water to a boil first, then two at a time with a slotted spoon slowly place eggs in boiling water (as many as you would like). Cover and let boil for 3 minutes. Turn heat off and keep covered for 15 more minutes.

Remove with the slotted spoon and let cool.

The shell will come right off and the yolk with be a perfect yellow (no brown outside).

Per 1 egg: 78 Calories; 6 g Protein; 1 g Carbohydrate; 1 g Sugar

OMG Clean Cut Eggvocado

- ½ of an avocado, pitted
- 1 egg
- Salt and Pepper to taste
- Get creative with toppings, crushed red pepper, Everything but the Bagel Sesame Seasoning, spices and seasonings

Preheat oven to 375° F.

Using a small piece of aluminum foil, create a 'boat' that will hold the avocado.

Scoop out a small amount of the avocado to create a larger hollow. Place avocado in your foil 'bowl' and crack the egg into the hollow. Top egg with salt and pepper and add seasonings of your choice. (Everything but the bagel seasoning is amazing on this!)

Bake until egg reaches desired doneness, about 15 minutes.

Makes 1 serving.

195 Calories; 8 g Protein; 7 g Carbohydrate; 5 g Fiber; 1 g Sugar; 16 g Fat

Canned Chicken Salad

- 4 small or 2 large cans of chunk chicken in water
- 1–2 tablespoons red wine vinegar
- Juice of one lemon or lime
- 2 tablespoons of real mayo (This is your fat.)
- 1–2 tablespoons of Honey cup mustard (red cap)
- 1 teaspoon of walnut oil (optional)
- Chopped fresh or dried rosemary
- Chopped fresh parsley (optional)
- Crushed almond or walnuts (optional)
- Chopped celery
- Pink sea salt and pepper to taste

Mix it all together and enjoy as a snack and a quick grab and go.

Makes 4 servings.

Per Serving: 183 Calories; 17 g Protein; 2.25 g Carbohydrate; 0.2 g, Sugar; 10 g Fat

Tuna Salad

- 4 small cans or 2 big cans of tuna (in water or oil) drained
- 1–2 tablespoons red wine vinegar
- Juice of one lime
- 2 tablespoons of real mayo (This is your fat.)
- 1–2 tablespoons of honey mustard
- Chopped celery
- Pink sea salt and pepper

Mix all together and you have a simple go-to.

Makes 4 servings.

Per serving: 82 Calories; 10 g Protein; 1.5 g Carbohydrate; 0.2 g Fiber; 0.2 g Sugar; 3.75 g Fat

Shredded Chicken and Salsa

This can be done in a crock pot or Instant Pot.

- 1 pound chicken breast
- 1 cup natural salsa
- 1 tablespoon cumin
- Himalayan Pink Salt and black pepper to taste

INSTANT POT:

Season chicken on both sides with spices. Place into the Instant Pot and cover with salsa.

Cook 20 minutes and use a natural release.

Once the Instant Pot releases the pressure, shred and enjoy!

CROCK POT:

Add all ingredients to crock pot and cook on high for 4–6 hours.

You can use this chicken in so many ways. Mix with cauliflower rice then after week one, you can add to brown rice, have with salads or in coconut wraps!

Makes 4 servings.

Per Serving: 142 Calories; 27 g Protein; 4 g Carbohydrate; 0.2 g Fiber; 2 g Sugar; 1.5 g Fat

Egg Roll in a Bowl

- 1 small head of cabbage, chopped into slices
- 2 large carrots, cut into long strips
- 1 onion sliced
- 1 tablespoon unflavored coconut oil
- ⅓ cup coconut aminos (optional)
- 1 tablespoon sesame oil
- 2 garlic cloves, minced
- 1 teaspoon fresh or ground ginger
- 4 green onions, diced for garnish
- 1 teaspoon soy sauce
- Pepper to taste
- Protein of choice—chicken and shrimp are best (or a ground meat)

Melt the coconut oil over medium high heat. Add the cabbage, carrots, and onions.

Sauté until soft. If it gets too dry, add a little water. Let it evaporate and help soften the veggies.

Add the coconut aminos and sesame oil.

Sauté until softer and the sauce is absorbed.

Add the garlic and ginger. Cook until fragrant.

Add the green onions on top.

Cook protein on the side, then toss with remainder of ingredients. Serve over cauliflower rice or zucchini noodles.

Makes 6 servings.

Per serving: 270 Calories; 10–15 g Protein; 8 g Carbohydrate; 6 g Sugar; 8–16 g Fat (depending on protein source)

Classic Clean Cut Shrimp and Peppers

- 1–2 pounds of shrimp, raw and cleaned (can buy frozen shrimp)
- 3 bell peppers (red, orange, and yellow) cut into ½ pieces
- Salt and pepper to taste
- 1 teaspoon paprika (to taste)
- 1–2 tablespoons of coconut oil or olive oil
- ¼ teaspoon garlic powder
- Dash of hot sauce

Place cleaned shrimp in bowl and add salt and pepper, paprika, garlic powder, and hot sauce mix and let sit in fridge or on counter. The juices from the shrimp will get expressed.

In a pan, add 1 tablespoon of olive oil and cook peppers for about 5–6 minutes (can add a bit of water if peppers need it). Add shrimp in one layer and cover for about 3–5 minutes. Flip shrimp and cook until tender. The juice from the peppers is all you need!

A serving is about 6 shrimp.

Per serving: 101 Calories; 11 g Protein; 6 g Carbohydrate; 3 g Sugar; 4.2 g Fat

Pesto Turkey or Chicken Meatballs

- 2 pounds ground turkey or chicken
- ½ cup almond or coconut flour
- ½ cup pesto
- 2 egg whites
- ½ teaspoon salt
- ¼ teaspoon freshly ground pepper

Preheat the oven to 375° F. Line a baking sheet with parchment paper (can place a wire cooling rack on top of the baking sheet to cook, or right on the tray).

In a large bowl, mix together all of the ingredients. Roll the mixture into small balls (about 1 inch each) using your hands and place on the wire rack or tray. Bake for 20–25 minutes, flipping halfway.

We like to keep these in fridge as a grab and go!

Serve over spaghetti squash or spiralized zucchini with a teaspoon of parmesan and a drizzle of olive oil.

Serving Size: 4 meatballs

Per serving: 270 Calories; 10–15 g Protein; 8 g Carbohydrate; 6 g Sugar; 8–16 g Fat

Butternut Squash Sauce

- ¼ cup raw cashews, soaked overnight or at least 3–4 hours
- 2 packages chopped squash
- ¾ cup water
- 2 garlic cloves
- 2 tablespoons nutritional yeast (optional, but recommended)
- 1 tablespoon fresh lemon juice
- ½ teaspoon onion powder
- ½ teaspoon smoked paprika
- ¼ teaspoon chili powder
- 1 teaspoon fine pink salt, or to taste
- Hot sauce, to taste

Drain cashews.

Preheat oven to 425° F and line a baking sheet with parchment paper.

Spread out chopped squash on sheet and drizzle with oil. Toss to coat. Sprinkle with salt. Roast for 30–40 minutes, flipping once halfway through, until squash is tender to the touch. Let cool for 5 minutes.

Add the soaked and drained cashews, water, garlic, nutritional yeast (if using), lemon juice, onion powder, paprika, chili powder, and 2 cups of cooked squash into a blender. Blend on high until smooth. Add the salt and hot sauce to taste and blend again.

Pour over roasted veggies or proteins. Leftover sauce can be stored in an airtight container for up to 1 week or so in the fridge.

Per serving: 75 Calories; 11 g Protein; 6 g Carbohydrate; 3 g Sugar; 4 g Fat

Sun-Dried Tomato Quiche

- 5 eggs
- 1 zucchini
- 1 onion
- ¼ teaspoon salt
- ¼ teaspoon pepper
- 2 teaspoons coconut oil
- 2 small tomatoes, sliced
- 4 ounces sun-dried tomatoes
- ¼ cup pancetta or ham, sliced

Preheat oven to 350° F.

Grease an 8-inch cast-iron skillet with 1 teaspoon coconut oil and set aside.

Melt 1 teaspoon coconut oil in a medium skillet over medium heat. Chop the onion and zucchini in a food processor until finely shredded, then cook in the skillet until soft and translucent, about 10 minutes.

While the zucchini and onions soften, drain the oil from your sun-dried tomatoes if you're using oil-packed. (If you don't like sun-dried tomato, you can substitute with any veggie you like). Roughly chop them and add to a medium mixing bowl.

Pull the pancetta or ham slices apart with your fingers like ripping them, then add to the tomatoes.

When the onions and zucchini are soft, add to the pancetta and tomatoes. Mix thoroughly and allow to cool to room temperature. Whisk in eggs, salt and pepper and pour into the cast-iron skillet for best results or the same pan you used for onions. Top with the slices of the two small tomatoes.

Cook in the preheated oven for 1 hour and 15 minutes or until firm.

Can cut pizza-like slices as breakfast or lunch with a nice salad. Stays in fridge nicely and it's an easy grab.

Makes 4 servings.

Per Serving: 216 Calories; 12 g Protein; 11 g Carbohydrate; 3 g Fat; 6.5 g Sugar; 12 g Fiber

Turkey Taco Stuffed Peppers

- 4 medium bell peppers (any color)
- 1 pound lean ground turkey (or lean ground beef)
- 2 tablespoons olive oil
- 2 teaspoons chili powder
- ½ teaspoon garlic powder
- ¼ teaspoon onion powder
- 1 teaspoon ground cumin
- ¼ teaspoon pink sea salt
- 1 can (4-ounce) diced green chilies
- 1 cup salsa

Toppings

- ½ cup tomato, diced (optional)
- 1 avocado chopped

Preheat oven to 350° F.

Spray a 9x9-inch baking dish with non-stick cooking spray. Wash peppers and cut around the stem to remove. Remove the seeds and ribs (whites) inside the peppers. Set peppers on baking pan.

Heat olive oil in pan to medium-high. Add the ground turkey, seasonings from chili powder to sea salt, and green chilies to the pan and mix. Cook until the meat is no longer pink. Add salsa to the skillet with the turkey and stir until everything is combined. Remove from heat. Spoon the turkey mixture evenly into the 4 peppers and sprinkle with diced tomatoes.

Bake, uncovered for 30–35 minutes, or until peppers are tender. Remove from the oven and top with chopped avocado.

Makes 4 servings.

Per serving: 354 Calories; 16.5 g Protein; 8.5 g Carbohydrate; 4.5 g Sugar; 6.25 g Fat

Cauliflower Rice

- "Rice" a head of cauliflower in the food processor, or use a pre- riced bag
- 1 cup of carrots in food processor
- 1 medium onion in food processor
- 1 tablespoon hot pepper sesame oil (if you want spicy or just plain sesame oil if not)
- 1 tablespoon of minced garlic
- 2 full eggs
- 2 egg whites scrambled
- 1 teaspoon chopped parsley
- 2 teaspoons orange zest
- ¼ teaspoon smoked paprika
- ½ teaspoon garlic powder
- salt and pepper to taste
- ¼ cup sesame seeds

Heat pan over medium to low heat, add the olive oil and sauté the garlic, then add the carrots and onion and cook for about 5–8 minutes (until they soften). Add the cauliflower, stirring for a few minutes.

Make a hole in center of pan (push cauliflower to sides and add the eggs to the middle). After the eggs are done, mix everything together in the pan. Then mix in the parsley, orange zest, paprika, and garlic powder, and drizzle with 1 teaspoon of sesame oil. Sprinkle with sesame seeds and enjoy.

Makes 4 servings.

Per Serving: 212 Calories; 13 g Protein; 18 g Carbohydrate; 7 g Fat; 8 g Sugar; 10 g Fiber

Rosemary Roasted Brussels Sprouts

- 2 pounds of Brussels sprouts, trimmed and halved
- 3 tablespoons fresh rosemary, chopped
- 1–1½ tablespoons olive oil
- 2 teaspoons balsamic vinegar
- ½ teaspoon sea salt and black pepper

Preheat oven to 425° F.

In a large bowl combine Brussels sprouts and rosemary. Top with olive oil and balsamic vinegar. Stir so all Brussels sprouts are coated. Spread evenly on a parchment-lined baking sheet. Sprinkle with sea salt and pepper to taste. Bake for 15 minutes Remove from oven and flip over. Bake for another 10 minutes. Serve warm.

Makes 4 servings.

Per serving: 100 Calories; 9.75 g Protein; 9.5 g Carbohydrate; 4.5 g Sugar; 5.75 g Fat

Sautéed Beet Greens and Spring Onions with Sherry Vinegar

- 1 bag of string beans
- 2 shallots (about ¼ cup)
- ½ to 1 teaspoon Irish butter
- Kosher or pink sea salt and pepper to taste
- ½–1 teaspoon sherry vinegar (depends on how much you like vinegar)

Trim beans if needed. Chop the shallots. Preheat a cast iron skillet or pan over medium heat. Add butter, and when it's hot, add, beans and shallots. Sauté about 5 minutes until softened. Season with a pinch of salt and pepper, then a drizzle of sherry vinegar. Serve warm or at room temperature.

Makes 2 servings.

Per Serving: 88 Calories; 2.5 g Protein; 11.5 g Carbohydrate; 4.5 g Fat; 3 g Sugar; 8 g Fiber

Clean Cut Detox Green Juice

- Huge handful of spinach or kale
- ½ bunch celery
- ½ bunch cilantro
- 1 cucumber with ends removed
- 1 lemon with peel removed
- 2 inches of fresh ginger root
- ¼ avocado

Blend all ingredients and enjoy.

Makes one serving.

Per serving: 100 Calories; 5 g Protein; 23 g Carbohydrate; 7 g Fiber; 8 g Sugar; 6 g Fat

---

CLEAN CUT TIP

Cut ripe avocado into quarters and freeze to use for your juice.

Vinaigrette

- 2 tablespoons olive oil
- 2 tablespoons balsamic vinegar
- 2 tablespoon honey mustard
- Juice of ½ a lime or the juice from grapefruit wedges
- Salt and pepper to taste

Two tablespoons is a serving.

Per serving: 146 Calories; 0g Protein; 10.6 g Carbohydrate; 10 g Sugar; 11 g Fat

Garlicky Herb Sauce

- 1 cup fresh flat-leaf parsley
- 1 cup fresh basil
- 1 garlic clove
- 1 tablespoon fresh lemon zest
- ⅓ cup extra-virgin olive oil
- ¼ teaspoon red pepper flakes
- Pink sea salt
- Freshly ground black pepper

Pulse parsley, basil, garlic, lemon zest, olive oil, and red pepper flakes in a food processor until finely chopped, 15 to 20 times. Season with pink sea salt and freshly ground black pepper.

Use to marinate chicken or fish or serve cold on top of anything you desire.

Makes 4 servings.

Per serving: 158 Calories; 0 g Protein; 0.25 g Carbohydrate; 0 g Sugar; 17 g Fat

Additional Fun Options for You to Start Creating

You can play with these foods to satisfy your taste.

Dijon mustard

Honey mustard

Lemon juice

Lime juice

Garlic clove

Pink sea salt

Miso broth

Chicken broth

Beef broth

Sesame oil

Cayenne pepper

Ground ginger

Cilantro

Raw organic honey

Salsa

Shallots

Sesame seeds

Any herbs, fresh or dried

Chili pepper

Cinnamon

Find Your Weekly Grocery Lists at www.cleancutfit.com/bookclub.

CHAPTER 7

Week 2

YAY! Week one is over!! Great work!!! To be successful you will need to follow what you have learned and listen to your body. Remember, it takes burning 3,500 excess calories to lose just 1 pound of fat—so keep moving.

IMPORTANT!

1. Continue to have a good fat with each meal (If you aren't hungry don't force it; listen to your body.)

2. Remember your portion sizes. Proteins should be fist-size. Fats as follows: half an avocado at a time, one full a day is great; nuts about eight to ten at a time; nut butters two teaspoons at a time. Limit nuts and nut butters to two servings per day. Veggies are always unlimited.

3. Do not forget your water. Adding in Himalayan Pink Salt helps hydrate you.

4. Pick something else to work on this week if you have conquered your first nemesis! Small PIVOTS lead to real change.

5. Let's talk about adding treats and cheats in this week.

Now that your detox week is over, you should have more energy and feel great. The fog should have lifted.

Week two doesn't change much. We are just adding in some bean options as they make a meal feel hearty. We are also going to talk about adding in a treat toward the end of the week along with alcohol. Be mindful and aware of how you feel when adding foods back in. You may find something you thought was great for you, actually doesn't make you feel all that good. This is important for your continued weight loss and lifestyle change. Remember to reach out if you have any questions at all.

Week 2

Thoughts

(Find a PDF copy at www.cleancutfit.com/bookclub)

Original weight week 1:

End of week 1 weight:

What were your takeaways from this week?

What worked?

What did you struggle with?

Go deep and be true to yourself.

Week 2

Education

Proven Health Benefits of Chia Seeds

Chia seeds are among the healthiest foods on the planet. They are loaded with nutrients that can have important benefits for your body and brain. Here are 5 health benefits of chia seeds that are supported by human studies.

1. Chia Seeds Deliver a Massive Amount of Nutrients with Very Few Calories

Chia seeds are tiny black seeds from the plant Salvia Hispanica, which is related to the mint family. This plant grows natively in South America. Chia seeds were an important food for the Aztecs and Mayans back in the day. They were prized for their ability to provide sustainable energy—in fact, "chia" is the ancient Mayan word for "strength." Despite their ancient history as a dietary staple, only recently did chia seeds become recognized as a modern-day superfood.

In the past few years, they have exploded in popularity and are now consumed by health-conscious people all over the world.

A one-ounce serving of chia seeds contains:

- Fiber: 11 grams
- Protein: 4 grams
- Fat: 9 grams (5 of which are Omega-3s)
- Calcium: 18% of the RDA
- Manganese: 30% of the RDA

- Magnesium: 30% of the RDA

- Phosphorus: 27% of the RDA

- They also contain a decent amount of Zinc, Vitamin B3 (Niacin), Potassium, Vitamin B1 (Thiamine) and Vitamin B2 (Riboflavin).

This nutrient profile is particularly impressive when you consider it is just for a single **ounce**, which supplies only 137 calories and one gram of digestible carbohydrate! Just so that we're all on the same page, one ounce equals 28 grams or about two tablespoons.

Bottom Line: Despite their tiny size, chia seeds are among the most nutritious foods on the planet. They are loaded with fiber, protein, Omega-3 fatty acids and various micronutrients.

2. Chia Seeds Are Loaded with Antioxidants

Although antioxidant *supplements* are not very effective, getting antioxidants from *foods* can have positive effects on health. Most importantly, antioxidants fight the production of free radicals, which can damage cells and contribute to ageing and diseases like cancer.

Bottom Line: Chia seeds are high in antioxidants that help to protect the delicate fats in the seeds. They also have various benefits for health.

3. Almost All the Carbs in Them Are Fiber

Looking at the nutrition profile of chia seeds, you see that an ounce has 12 grams of "carbohydrate." However, 11 of those grams are fiber, which isn't digested by the body. Fiber doesn't raise blood sugar, doesn't require insulin to be secreted and therefore shouldn't count as a carb. Because of all the fiber, chia seeds can absorb up to 10–12 times their weight in water, becoming gel-like and expanding in the stomach. Theoretically, this should increase fullness, slow absorption of food and help you eat fewer calories. Fiber also feeds the friendly bacteria in the intestine, which is important because keeping the gut microbiome well fed is crucial for health. Chia seeds are 40% fiber by weight, making them one of the best sources of fiber in the world.

Bottom Line: Almost all of the carbohydrates in chia seeds are fiber. This gives them the ability to absorb 10–12 times their weight in water. Fiber also has various beneficial effects on health.

4. Chia Seeds Are High in Quality Protein

Chia seeds contain a decent amount of protein. By weight, they are about 14% protein, which is very high compared to most plants. They also contain a good balance of essential amino acids, so our bodies should be able to make use of the protein in them. Protein has all sorts of benefits for health. It is also the most weight loss–friendly nutrient in the diet, **by far**.

Bottom Line: Chia seeds are high in quality protein, much higher than most plant foods. Protein is the most weight loss–friendly macronutrient and can drastically reduce appetite and cravings.

5. Due to the High Fiber and Protein Content, Chia Seeds Should be Able to Help You Lose Weight

Many health experts believe that chia seeds can help with weight loss. The fiber absorbs large amounts of water and expands in the stomach, which should increase fullness and slow the absorption of food. Then the protein in chia seeds could help to reduce appetite and food intake. Although, *just* adding chia seeds to your diet is unlikely to affect your weight.

Bottom Line: Chia seeds are high in protein and fiber, both of which have been shown to aid weight loss.

Week 2 Menu Guide

Day 1		
Breakfast	**Lunch**	**Dinner**
Black bean spinach quiche **OR** Two scrambled eggs with ½ an avocado (mashed) wrapped in a turmeric coconut wrap with pink salt to taste	Avocado Egg Mash: This is extremely versatile and can be made to your taste. Half avocado, 2 hard-boiled eggs all mashed with a little Dijon mustard, pink salt and lemon juice. Season to taste and get creative! Use veggies to dip or spoon onto mushroom caps.	Coco Chili (see recipes)
Snack	**Snack**	**Snack**
2 teaspoons nut butter **OR** 10 raw nuts	Veggies ¼ cup hummus	5 walnuts with ½ teaspoon melted Irish butter with cinnamon sprinkled on top

Day 2		
Breakfast	**Lunch**	**Dinner**
2 hard-boiled eggs with veggies (salsa or hot sauce) **OR** eggs anyway with ½ an avocado **OR** 2 egg cups **OR** Slice of quiche (about ⅛ is a serving)	Leftover chili from dinner	Spaghetti Squash with Kale and Bacon (see recipes), can add any grilled, baked or roasted protein
Snack	**Snack**	**Snack**
3 turkey roll-ups with mustard or hot sauce with a few slices of avocado **OR** 4–5 coconut chucks	Make one of the side salads in bulk and use for snack or add to lunch throughout week	1 tablespoon nut butter

Day 3

Breakfast	Lunch	Dinner
Avocado Pudding (see recipes) **OR** Green Juice (see recipe)	Tuna or chicken salad wrapped in coconut wrap with half a smashed avocado with big salad **OR** Leftovers from dinner	Easy Shredded Chicken Tacos (see recipes)
Snack	**Snack**	**Snack**
8–10 nuts **OR** 2 teaspoons nut butter **OR** Coconut chunks	Veggies with salsa or honey mustard **OR** 2 hard-boiled eggs with salt and pepper	4 ounces turkey meat rolled with honey or Dijon mustard

Day 4

Breakfast	Lunch	Dinner
Green Juice **OR** Any of the egg options	Leftover chicken taco over big salad with ½ an avocado **OR** The "avocado and egg mash" from day one	One-Pot Greek Chicken (see recipes)
Snack	**Snack**	**Snack**
8 nuts **OR** 2 teaspoons nut butter	Side salad option	2 teaspoons nut butter **OR** Coconut chunks

Day 5

Breakfast	Lunch	Dinner
Egg cups **OR** One slice of either quiche topped with ½ an avocado	Leftover chicken with one of the side salads	Shrimp Tacos (see recipes)with Roasted Garlic Cauliflower (see recipes)
Snack	**Snack**	**Snack**
2 teaspoons of nut butter	1 cup chopped veggies with hummus	Crispy Roasted Chickpeas (see recipes)

Day 6

Breakfast	Lunch	Dinner
Sun-dried tomato quiche **OR** Black bean quiche	Leftover shrimp Tacos **OR** Slice of quiche with ½ avocado and side salad	Slow-cooked black bean chicken with side of cauliflower rice (from week one)
Snack	**Snack**	**Snack**
4 slices of turkey rolled with canned roasted peppers and mustard of choice	Roasted chickpeas	1 tablespoon nut butter

Day 7		
Breakfast	**Lunch**	**Dinner**
Green Juice **OR** Any of the egg choices	Leftover chicken from day 6 **OR** Tuna or chicken salad in coconut wrap	Vegetarian Sun-Dried Tomato Basil Balls (or use ground turkey, chicken, or lean beef with same recipe) (see recipes) with steamed asparagus drizzled with olive oil plus sea salt and pepper
Snack	**Snack**	**Snack**
Handful of nuts **OR** Coconut chunks	Turkey roll-ups with hummus	Sliced avocado with a drizzle of olive or sesame oil and choice of seasoning

Recipes

Black Bean Spinach Quiche

- 6 Eggs
- ½ cup chopped onion
- 2 cup chopped spinach
- 1 juicy tomato, sliced (your choice!)
- 2 tablespoons plus 1 teaspoon olive oil, divided
- 1 tablespoon fresh lime juice
- ¾ teaspoon chili powder
- ½ teaspoon Himalayan Pink Salt
- ½ teaspoon ground cumin
- 1 can low-sodium black beans, drained

Heat oven to 375° F.

In bowl mix the lime, chili powder, salt, cumin, and black beans.

Heat a skillet with 1 tablespoon of olive oil and sauté the onion and spinach.

Beat the eggs.

Add the bean mixture to pan and heat through until beans are soft, about 5 minutes (stirring often)

Add the eggs and mix evenly. Place in oven for 30 minutes, then add tomato slices on top and bake for another 10 minutes.

Makes 4 servings.

Per serving: 282 Calories; 17 g Protein; 20 g Carbohydrate; 2.75 g Sugar; 15 g Fat

Avocado Pudding Breakfast

- 1 ripe avocado
- ½ cup unsweetened almond milk
- 1 tablespoon honey
- 1 tablespoon cacao powder
- 2 to 3 tablespoons crushed almonds

Blend avocado, milk, and honey in a blender (or food processor) until smooth. Garnish with almonds. You can also chill for about an hour for a refreshing treat.

One avocado is one serving.

Per serving: 397 Calories; 7 g Protein; 36 g Carbohydrate; 18 g Sugar; 28 g Fat

Easy Shredded Chicken Tacos

- 3 cups cabbage slaw mix
- 1 cup loosely packed fresh cilantro leaves
- 1¼ cups red or green salsa, divided
- 1 can (8-ounce) black beans (These are very high in fiber, so the net ratio of carbs is lower.)
- ¼ teaspoon ground cumin or low sodium taco seasoning
- Salt and pepper (if not using taco seasoning)
- 2 cups shredded chicken breast meat from an organic rotisserie chicken
- Bib lettuce

In a large bowl, toss slaw mix, cilantro and ¾ cup salsa. Set aside.

In a saucepan, combine beans, cumin/taco seasoning, and a pinch of salt and pepper. Heat over medium heat 3 to 5 minutes, or until hot, stirring occasionally. Fold in chicken.

Use the leaf of the bib lettuce as your shell; top with salsa.

Makes 3 servings.

Per serving: 363 Calories; 34 g Protein; 35 g Carbohydrate; 8 g Sugar; 4 g Fat

Spaghetti Squash with Kale and Bacon

- 1 small to medium spaghetti squash
- ½ tablespoon olive oil
- Himalayan Pink Salt to taste
- 2 slices of bacon
- 2 tablespoons minced shallot
- 1 clove garlic, minced
- 1 cup kale leaves cut into skinny threads (called a chiffonade)
- 1 teaspoon apple cider vinegar
- ¼ teaspoon black pepper

CLEAN CUT SQUASH HINT!

Poke some holes in the squash with a knife, then put squash in the microwave for a few minutes at a time until it softens a bit for easier cutting! (Save a finger!)

Preheat the oven to 375° F. Cut squash in half vertically and scoop out seeds. Coat with olive oil and generous amount of pink salt.

Place cut side down on a baking sheet lined with parchment paper and roast for 12 minutes. Turn over and bake for another 15–20 minutes. When the strands pull away from the skin, it is done. It should be al dente like pasta. Remove from oven and use a fork to remove the strands. Drain squash on a paper towel.

While squash is roasting, cook bacon on stove. Cook until crispy or to your liking. Remove bacon and drain on paper towel. Once it is cool make it into a crumble.

Keep about 1 tablespoon bacon grease and clean the rest out of the pan. Add shallots and garlic to pan and sauté over medium heat for 3 minutes, until translucent (careful not to burn).

Stir in kale and a little water if needed to help wilt. Cook for 4–5 minutes.

Add the spaghetti squash to the pan and gently combine. Stir in bacon, vinegar, black pepper, and more salt to taste. If you like it a little crispy once blended leave it for 2–3 minutes then toast again for remaining time.

Makes 2 servings.

Per serving: 170 Calories; 4.5 g Protein; 21.5 g Carbohydrate; 8.5 g Sugar; 9 g Fat

Coco Chili

- 2 tablespoons coconut oil or Irish butter
- 2 medium onions, diced (about 2 cups)
- 4 cloves garlic, minced (about 4 teaspoons)
- 2 pounds ground beef
- 1 teaspoon dried oregano leaves
- 2 tablespoons chili powder
- 2 tablespoons cacao powder
- 1 teaspoon ground allspice
- 1 teaspoon Pink salt
- 1 can (6ounce) tomato paste
- 1 can (14.5-ounce) fire-roasted, chopped tomatoes
- 2 cups chicken or beef broth
- 1 cup water

Heat a large, deep pot over medium-high heat, then add the coconut oil or butter. When the oil or butter has melted, add onions, cook until they're translucent, about 7 minutes. Add the garlic for about 30 seconds, then add the beef and crumble it up and mix together.

Continue to cook the meat, stirring often, until it's no longer pink.

In a small bowl, crush the oregano to release its flavor, add the chili powder, cacao, allspice, and pink salt. Then add to the pot and mix well. Add tomato paste and stir until combined, about 2 minutes.

Add the tomatoes with their juice, broth, and water and stir well. Bring to a boil, then reduce the heat to a gentle simmer. Simmer uncovered for 30 minutes to an hour.

Makes 8 servings.

Per serving: 323 Calories; 24.5 g Protein; 8.75 g Carbohydrate; 4 g Sugar; 20.5 g Fat

One Pot Greek Chicken and Tomatoes

Tomatoes

- 2 tablespoons olive oil
- 4 cloves garlic crushed
- 2 tablespoons crushed red pepper flakes
- 2 heirloom tomatoes sliced or any tomato of your choice
- 2 cups heirloom cherry tomatoes halved or cherry tomato of choice
- salt and pepper to taste

Chicken

- 2 tablespoons olive oil
- 1 pound boneless, skinless chicken, cut into bite size pieces
- 2–3 cloves garlic minced or grated
- 2 tablespoons balsamic vinegar
- 1 tablespoon smoked paprika
- ½ teaspoon salt + pepper
- ½ cup fresh oregano chopped (dried is OK)
- 2 bell peppers sliced
- 1 cup mixed Kalamata or green olives

Tomatoes

Add olive oil, garlic and chili pepper flakes to a small saucepan. Heat on low. Simmer for 20–30 minutes and then remove from the heat. Allow to cool.

This can be stored in a glass jar for up to a month in the fridge. Can be used as a side to most dishes.

Chicken

Toss the chicken with the garlic, vinegar, paprika, salt and pepper. Heat 2 tablespoons olive oil in a large skillet set on medium-high heat. Once hot, add the chicken. Cook until the chicken is browned all over and cooked through, about 5 minutes. Stir in the oregano and cook another minute. Remove the chicken from the pan and to a plate.

To the same pan, add another tablespoon of olive oil, the bell peppers, and a pinch of salt + pepper. Sear the peppers until just beginning to caramelize on the edges, about 3–4 minutes. Add the olives and chicken back in and toss for about 2 minutes.

Serve over the tomatoes.

Makes 4 servings.

Per serving: 341 Calories; 27.5 g Protein; 16 g Carbohydrate; 10 g Sugar; 18.25 g Fat

Shrimp Tacos

- 1 tablespoon olive oil
- 1 tablespoon chili powder
- 1 teaspoon salt
- 1 pound medium shrimp, peeled, deveined and clean
- 1 avocado, pitted and diced
- Shredded lettuce, for serving (can buy in grocery store)
- Fresh cilantro, for serving
- 1 lime, cut into wedges

Use coconut wraps (can be found at most health food stores) or lettuce wraps.

Heat a skillet to medium-high. Mix together the olive oil, chili powder, and salt and toss with the shrimp to coat. Cook in the skillet for 1–2 minutes per side, until pink. Set aside.

Top each wrap with cooked shrimp, shredded lettuce, avocado, and cilantro. Serve with a lime wedge.

Makes 4 servings.

Without coconut wrap:

Per serving: 209 Calories; 26 g Protein; 3 g Carbohydrate; 1 g Sugar; 10.5 g Fat

With coconut wrap: 279 Calories; 27 g Protein: 9 g Carbohydrate: 4 g Sugar: 15.5 g Fat

Cut Slow Cooker
hwestern Black Bean Chicken

- 1 pound boneless, skinless chicken breasts
- 1 can pinto beans or black beans, rinsed and drained (organic)
- 1 can (28-ounce) diced tomatoes in juice (low sodium is best)
- 1 bag organic spinach
- 1 container of your favorite salsa, no sugar added

Place the chicken breasts on the bottom of your slow cooker.

Pour the tomatoes and salsa over the chicken, then layer on the beans and spinach.

Cook on low for 5–7 hours, or until the chicken easily falls apart when the pot is stirred.

Serve with Crunchy Tomato Salad

Makes 4 Servings.

Per serving: 256 Calories; 33 g Protein; 28 g Carbohydrate; 6.5 g Sugar; 1.25 g Fat

Vegetarian Sun-Dried Tomato Basil Balls

- 1 egg
- 1 tablespoon flaxseed meal
- 2 ½ tablespoons water
- 2 tablespoons olive oil, divided, plus more for sautéing
- 3 cloves garlic minced
- ⅓ cup almond or coconut flour
- ⅓ cup loosely packed fresh basil, chopped
- ⅓ cup loosely packed chopped sun-dried tomatoes (dry, not in oil)
- Pinch of sea salt and red pepper flakes, more if you like spicy
- 1 can (15-ounce) chickpeas, drained, rinsed and dried

Preheat oven to 375 degrees. Heat a large metal or cast-iron skillet over medium heat.

Add 1 tablespoon of olive oil and minced garlic. Sauté until lightly browned, stirring often—about 3 minutes. Remove from heat and cool slightly, In food processor blend egg, flour, water, basil, sun-dried tomatoes, salt, red pepper flakes, and 1 tablespoon olive oil. Pulse/blend until small bits remain, scraping down sides as needed.

Next add rinsed/dried chickpeas and blend/pulse until a moldable "dough" is formed. You don't want the chickpeas to turn into a paste, but you also don't want any left whole.

Taste and adjust seasonings as needed. Scoop out rounded 1-tablespoon amounts of dough and gently form/roll into balls—about 15 total.

Heat the same skillet you used earlier over medium heat. Once hot, add enough olive oil to form a thin layer on the bottom of the skillet, about 2 tablespoons. Then add meatballs in two batches, no crowding.

Brown for about 5 minutes total, rolling them over. Turn down heat slightly if browning too quickly.

Add sautéed meatballs to a parchment paper–lined baking sheet, transfer to the preheated oven and bake for 15 minutes.

Leftover meatballs will keep in the refrigerator for 3–4 days, though best when fresh. Reheat in the microwave or in a 350-degree oven until warmed through.

Make 2 Servings.

Per serving: 365 Calories; 18.5 g Protein; 52 g Carbohydrate; 5 g Sugar; 24 g Fat

Roasted Garlic Cauliflower (side dish)

- 1 head cauliflower
- ¼ cup coconut oil, melted
- 4 cloves garlic, minced
- Himalayan Pink Salt and freshly ground black pepper, to taste
- 2 tablespoons chopped fresh parsley leaves

Preheat oven to 425° F.

Lightly oil a baking sheet or coat with nonstick spray. Place cauliflower florets in a single layer onto the prepared baking sheet.

Add coconut oil and garlic; season with salt and pepper, to taste. Gently toss to combine.

Place into oven and bake for 12–14 minutes, or until tender and golden brown.

Sprinkle with parsley, if desired.

Makes 4 servings.

Per serving: 172.5 Calories; 4.25 g Protein; 11.25 g Carbohydrate; 5 g Sugar; 21 g Fat

Crispy Roasted Chickpeas

- 2 cans (15-ounce) chickpeas

- 2 tablespoons olive oil

- ½ to ¾ teaspoon salt

2 to 4 teaspoons spices or finely chopped fresh herbs (chili powder, curry powder, cinnamon, garlic, cumin, smoked paprika, rosemary, thyme, or other favorite spices and herbs) Get Creative!

Heat oven to 400° F.

Pour chickpeas in a strainer to rinse and drain. Lay paper towels or dish towel on a baking sheet and pour beans out onto the towel to dry for a bit. I usually leave them about an hour.

Toss chickpeas in a bowl with olive oil (or the oil of your choice) and salt. Make sure they are evenly coated. Add the seasoning of your choice. Do not add too much as the seasoning sometimes burns if too much is added. You can always toss with more once done cooking.

Lay the chickpeas on a baking sheet and bake for 20–30 minutes depending on oven. Check every 10 minutes or so, and toss as needed.

Toss with more seasoning if needed. These are a great snack. As they cool, they sometimes get chewy. Still delish! You can also use these as croutons on a salad for a crunch!

Makes 3 Servings.

Per serving: 220 Calories; 7 g Protein; 23 g Carbohydrate; 0 g Sugar; 20 g Fat

Salad in A Blender (Green Juice)

- Huge handful of spinach or kale
- ½ bunch celery
- ½ bunch cilantro
- 1 cucumber with ends removed
- 1 lemon with peel removed
- 2 inches of fresh ginger root

Build Your Immunity

- 1 cup coconut water
- 2 romaine lettuce leaves
- ¼ cucumber
- ¼ avocado, peeled
- ½ lemon
- ½ inch ginger
- ½ cup parsley
- The contents of 1 probiotic capsule (OPTIONAL)

Refresh!

- 1 ½ cup coconut water
- ½ cup kale
- ½ cup spinach
- ½ cup romaine lettuce
- ⅓ lime, peeled
- Leaves from 2 stems of mint

CHAPTER 8

Week 3

What is your weight this week?

What are your takeaways this week?

What was your biggest challenge?

Did you conquer any nemesis?

Did you notice anything that gave you energy or created a sluggish feeling? GO DEEP!

This week, we want you to work on consistency, and your CHOICES. We want you to figure out what works for you and be satisfied. FIND THOSE GO-TO FOODS!

Welcome to week 3—the week you've been waiting for because it includes COMPLEX CARBS AND SOME FRUIT. **You can have a serving a day or even every other day if you want to reintroduce more slowly.** You can have the serving all at one time or broken up during the day. It can be ½ a serving of a complex carb and a

½ serving of fruit to equal one serving. It can be a full serving of a carbs at one time or broken up. The same goes for fruit. See the serving size chart below.

For Example:

Monday: One full piece of sprouted bread is your serving for the day.

Tuesday: One full apple broken up into two snacks is your serving for the day.

Wednesday: Two ½ servings of fruit make up your serving.

COMPLEX CARBS ALLOWED: (½ cup cooked grains)

Brown Rice (only on sushi for now)

Oatmeal (gluten-free and limit)

Quinoa

Sweet Potato (1 cup cubed)

Sprouted bread (1 slice)

FRUITS:

Cherries

Apples

Strawberries

Blueberries

Grapes

Grapefruit

Note: Please stay away from bananas for now **unless you are using them specifically for a pre-workout or a specific reason.** Post questions about this on our website.

Week 3

Education

Creative options for new habits!!

Maybe you've used some of these already but here are some more:

- Mashed avocado for butter on sprouted toast
- Nuts for croutons in salad
- Seltzer water for tonic water
- Alternative flour (coconut, almond, etc.) for white flour
- Zucchini "ribbons" or spaghetti squash for pasta
- Pureed potato, butternut squash for cream in soup
- Natural peanut butter for reduced-fat peanut butter
- Stevia for sugar (if you like it) 1 cup sugar is equal to 1 teaspoon of liquid stevia or 2 tablespoons of Stevia powder or real raw honey or agave (1 teaspoon)
- Mashed cauliflower or squash or cauliflower rice for mashed potatoes or rice
- Crushed flax or fiber cereal for bread crumbs
- Nutritional yeast for cheese
- Coconut wrap, lettuce leaves or collard greens for tortilla wraps
- Himalayan Pink Salt for regular salt
- Seltzer water with citrus slices instead of soda

Week 3 Menu Guide

Day 1		
Breakfast	**Lunch**	**Dinner**
½ avocado mashed with one full egg on sprouted **OR** Gluten-free toast with crushed red pepper and pink salt	Herb Tuna Salad (½ cup) (see recipe) with unlimited veggies	Stuffed Portobello Mushrooms (see recipes) Salad or veggie of choice
Snack	**Snack**	**Snack**
Your go-to morning snack	Half an avocado with pink salt and pepper and a squeeze of lime with cherry tomatoes	Handful of nuts

Day 2		
Breakfast	**Lunch**	**Dinner**
Eggs anyway you like them with tons of veggies **OR** Your "go-to" breakfast that has been working for you (like egg cups)	Leftover stuffed mushrooms (can add a fried egg, yum!)	Zucchini Cilantro Turkey Burgers (see recipes) with veggie mash
Snack	**Snack**	**Snack**
Crispy Roasted Chickpeas **OR** your "go-to" snack	½ of an apple with nut butter **OR** 1–2 hard-boiled eggs with hot sauce	2 teaspoons nut butter

Day 3

Breakfast	Lunch	Dinner
1 plain 2% or 4% Greek yogurt with ½ cup of berries	Shredded chicken wrap (another fun way to create your own meal!) Boil, slow cook or use all natural rotisserie chicken breasts. Shred and use about 4 ounces. Use a green leaf or a coconut wrap. Spread hummus or avocado and use unlimited veggies! We use cucumber, red bell pepper, spinach, etc. We also have added some olives or jalapenos! Add a little feta (optional, fingertip-full).	Protein of your choice with side of veggie mash (see recipes) **OR** Cauliflower Steak
Snack	**Snack**	**Snack**
½ a coconut wrap with 1 teaspoon nut butter	½ Apple with 2 teaspoons of nut butter	Rice crackers dipped in mashed avocado

Day 4		
Breakfast	**Lunch**	**Dinner**
Egg Cups **OR** Egg quiche	Chicken salad or herb tuna salad over greens (unlimited veggies) **OR** Protein with ½ cup of veggie mash	One Pot Chicken and Quinoa (see recipes)
Snack	**Snack**	**Snack**
Turkey and avocado wraps Use 3–4 Slices of turkey. Slice some avocado and roll the avocado up in the turkey.	Roasted chickpeas **OR** Your afternoon "go-to"	2 squares of good dark chocolate (Yes, we said it!)

Day 5

Breakfast	Lunch	Dinner
Oatmeal Protein Pancakes	Leftover quinoa (½ cup only) with one fried egg and cherry tomatoes	Chicken or Shrimp Stir Fry (see recipe)
Snack	**Snack**	**Snack**
Black Bean Hummus and veggies **OR** Your "go-to"	Protein Shake **OR** Green Juice	Lean protein **OR** handful of nuts

Day 6

Breakfast	Lunch	Dinner
Sprouted toast with ½ avocado smash with scrambled eggs **OR** Coconut wrap with 2 teaspoons nut butter and sliced berries rolled up	Leftover stir fry **OR** Your "go-to"	Chicken with Apple and Sage (see recipes)
Snack	**Snack**	**Snack**
Chicken or Tuna Salad (week 1- or 3-type) in ½ a coconut wrap	2 teaspoons nut butter	Cherry Smoothie (see recipes)

Day 7		
Breakfast	**Lunch**	**Dinner**
Oatmeal Protein Pancakes	Leftovers	Squash and Tomato Spiced (see recipes)
Snack	**Snack**	**Snack**
10 nuts	Protein Shake **OR** Your "go-to" snack	Lean Protein **OR** ½ of your yogurt with cinnamon and 5 nuts (can crush them)

Recipes

Stuffed Portobello Mushrooms (vegan)

(If you are non-vegan, you can add any kind of protein.)

- 8 baby Portobello mushroom caps or 4 large, stems removed
- 2–3 links natural chicken sausage (optional; any health store carries all sorts of flavors)
- 1 avocado
- 1 small handful baby kale or spinach leaves
- ¼ cup fresh basil (optional)
- ½ juice of fresh lime juice
- ½ teaspoon garlic powder
- Himalayan Pink Salt to taste

Either grill or sauté the mushroom and chicken sausage (if using). Mushrooms should be tender not soft. Cook sausage until heated through.

Dice the avocado and mix with the kale or spinach, lime juice, garlic, and salt. Crumble the sausage (if using) and add to avocado mix. Place in each mushroom cap.

Makes 4 servings.

Per serving: 180 Calories; 12 g Protein; 14 g Carbohydrate; 5 g Sugar; 10 g Fat (Calories will vary if adding protein)

Zucchini Cilantro Turkey Burgers

- 1 pound lean ground turkey
- 1 cup shredded zucchini, after liquid squeezed out (approx. 1 small zucchini) Be sure to squeeze out liquid.
- 1 small onion, pureed or grated
- 1 small garlic clove, crushed or grated
- ¼ teaspoon sea salt
- ¼ teaspoon ground black pepper
- 1 tablespoon cumin (optional)
- ¼ cup cilantro, finely chopped
- Juice from ½ a lime
- 12 lettuce leaves
- 12 tomato slices
- 12 red onion slices

For Cilantro Aioli:

- ½ cup Greek yogurt, plain
- ¼ cup cilantro, finely chopped
- 2 celery sticks finely chopped
- 2 teaspoons jalapeño pepper, finely diced (or to taste)
- Other half of the lime, juiced
- 1 teaspoon garlic powder
- Pinch of salt
- Pinch of ground black pepper

Line baking sheet with parchment paper. Combine turkey patty ingredients in a medium bowl and mix. Form into 6 round patties

½ inch thick, place on a baking sheet, cover with plastic wrap and refrigerate for at least an hour. It helps the patties to stay together.

In a small bowl, combine cilantro aioli ingredients, mix, cover and refrigerate.

Preheat grill on medium and spray with cooking spray. Spray turkey patties on both sides with cooking spray, place on a grill and cook for 6–8 minutes, flipping halfway through. Grills vary, so check your burger for doneness by inserting a food thermometer into the center of the patty.

Cook until thermometer reads 165 degrees.

Place lettuce leaf down, add burger, and top with onion tomato and a tablespoon of aioli. Cover with another piece of lettuce and enjoy!

Makes 4-6 servings.

Per burger: 175 Calories; 23 g Protein; 4 g Carbohydrate; 2 g Sugar; 8 g Fat

Aioli: 47 Calories; 6 g Protein; 7 g Carbohydrate; 3 g Sugar

One Pot Chicken and Quinoa

- 2 pounds boneless, skinless chicken breasts, cut into 1 inch pieces
- 1 tablespoon olive oil
- ½ teaspoon ground ginger
- ½ teaspoon allspice (optional but good)
- ½ teaspoon sea salt
- Ground black pepper, to taste

Quinoa:

- 2 medium onions, diced
- 3 large garlic cloves, minced
- 1 large carrot, shredded
- 2 sticks celery chopped
- 1 teaspoon olive oil
- 1½ cups quinoa, uncooked
- 3 cups boiling water
- ¾ teaspoon sea salt
- 2 bay leaves
- 1 pound broccoli, chopped

Preheat large skillet or Dutch oven to medium high heat.

Add the chicken and all the ingredients from olive oil to black pepper. Stir occasionally. Cook until browned. If too much liquid is in pan, drain some. Transfer to a bowl and set aside.

Add olive oil, onions, garlic, carrot, celery and cook for 3–5 minutes, stirring occasionally. Add pre-cooked chicken, quinoa, water, remaining salt, and bay leaves; stir. Bring to a boil, cover, reduce heat to low and cook for 20 minutes.

At this point quinoa should be cooked al dente. Add broccoli, stir, cover and cook for 5 more minutes. Serve hot.

Makes 6 servings.

Per serving: 311 Calories; 27 g Protein; 37 g Carbohydrate; 7 g Sugar; 7 g Fat

Squash and Tomato Spiced

- 1 tablespoon of olive or coconut oil
- 1 red or sweet onion, chopped
- 2 small squash of choice (yellow, butternut, acorn) cut in ½ pieces (Butternut usually comes chopped already.)
- 1–2 cloves of garlic
- 1 jalapeño or poblano (smoky flavor)
- Himalayan Pink Salt to taste (about 1 teaspoon)
- 1 can (28-ounce) diced tomatoes (organic)

Heat the oil in a skillet over medium heat. Once hot, add the onion and season with some salt. Cook for a few minutes (until translucent) then add the squash, garlic, pepper, and more salt. Cook until squash starts to become tender (4 or so minutes) then add the diced tomato along with the juice. Cover and simmer on low for about 10-12 minutes.

Can add any protein of choice to the simmering squash. Season with pepper, cook protein through, and serve.

Makes 3 servings.

Per serving: 154 Calories; 3 g Protein; 20 g Carbohydrate; 7 g Sugar; 9 g Fat

Black Bean Hummus

- 1 clove garlic
- 1 (15-ounce) can black beans, drained and rinsed
- 1 tablespoon olive oil
- 2 tablespoons lemon juice
- 1½ tablespoons tahini
- ¾ teaspoon ground cumin
- ½ teaspoon salt
- ¼ teaspoon cayenne pepper
- ¼ teaspoon paprika

Mince garlic in the bowl of a food processor.

Add black beans, olive oil, 2 tablespoons lemon juice, tahini, ½ teaspoon cumin, ½ teaspoon salt, and ⅛ teaspoon cayenne pepper; process until smooth, scraping down the sides as needed.

Add additional seasoning and water to taste and desired texture. Garnish with paprika.

Makes 3 servings.

Per serving: 226 Calories; 9 g Protein; 21 g Carbohydrate; 1 g Sugar; 13 g Fat

Vegetarian Cauliflower "Steaks"

- 2 large heads of cauliflower
- 3 tablespoon olive oil plus additional for drizzling
- 2 teaspoons smoked paprika, divided
- ½ teaspoon ground black pepper
- ¼ teaspoon Pink Himalayan salt plus additional as needed
- 2 garlic cloves finely chopped (more to taste)
- 1–2 cups organic diced tomatoes
- 2 cups spinach
- 1 teaspoon sesame seeds, toasted

Preheat oven to 425°F. Line baking sheet with foil and spray.

Trim the stems of cauliflower heads so that cauliflower sits flat upright. Cut each cauliflower vertically into two, ¾-inch-thick steaks, making 4 steaks total.

In a bowl, mix together oil, 1 teaspoon paprika, pepper, salt and garlic. Brush half of mixture over cauliflower. Roast for 10 minutes. Turn the steaks over and brush with remaining oil mixture. Roast until tender and golden brown, about 25 minutes.

In a small saucepan, combine diced tomato, spinach, remaining 1 teaspoon smoked paprika and additional salt as needed; heat on low until warmed.

Pour sauce over steaks when serving and add some sesame seeds (optional) on top.

Makes 4 servings.

Per serving: 184 Calories; 10 g Protein; 25 g Carbohydrate; 12 g Sugar; 7 g Fat

Oatmeal Protein Pancakes

- 1–2 cups oats (depends on how thick you like them)
- 1 cup Greek yogurt
- Pink salt to taste
- 1 teaspoon baking powder
- 3 eggs
- 1 teaspoon vanilla extract
- Water to desired thickness
- Cinnamon and/or nutmeg (optional)

Mix all ingredients. Add water to desired thickness. You can put in blender and pulse or smooth to your taste. Cook on griddle and enjoy!

Makes 4 pancakes.

Per serving: 391 Calories; 23 g Protein; 54 g Carbohydrate; 2 g Sugar; 10 g Fat

Chicken or Shrimp Stir Fry

- 1 tablespoon olive oil
- 4 eggs, large
- 1 tablespoon Irish butter
- 1 pound mushrooms, sliced
- 2 teaspoons soy sauce
- 1 pound boneless, skinless chicken breasts, cut into 0.5-inch pieces or 1 pound cleaned shrimp
- ½ inch fresh ginger, grated
- 1 garlic clove, crushed
- 1 teaspoon sesame oil
- 1 large bell pepper, cut into 1-inch pieces
- 1 extra-large zucchini, cut into 1-inch pieces
- 1 large head broccoli (including stems), cut into 1-inch pieces

Heat oil in pan or wok over medium-high heat.

Add the eggs. Stir often to make scrambled eggs. Transfer to a large bowl. Increase heat to high and add Irish butter, mushrooms, and soy sauce; cook until golden brown, stirring frequently. Transfer to the bowl with eggs.

Return skillet to high heat, add another tablespoon olive oil. Add chicken along with the 2 teaspoons soy sauce, ½ inch ginger, garlic, and sesame oil. Cook until a bit golden brown, stirring occasionally. Transfer to the same bowl. If using shrimp, wait until the end to put them in.

Return skillet to high heat. Add peppers, zucchini, broccoli, other ½ inch ginger, garlic, and the soy sauce and cook until golden brown but still firm, stirring frequently. Transfer to a bowl with other ingredients.

Return skillet to high heat and add 1 tablespoon coconut oil. If using shrimp, cook, them now (about 3–4 minutes each side). Transfer previously cooked ingredients from a bowl to the skillet; mix and heat through.

Makes 6 servings.

Per serving: with chicken: 390 Calories; 47 g Protein; 15 g Carbohydrate; 5 g Sugar; 18 g Fat

Per serving: with shrimp: 260 Calories; 12 g Protein 15 g Carbohydrate; 5 g Sugar; 16 g Fat

Mashed Roasted Veggies

- 1 head roasted garlic (Chop off the top, drizzle with olive oil and pink salt, wrap in aluminum foil and bake at 350° F for about 45 minutes.)
- 3 tablespoons of Irish butter
- ½ onion, finely chopped
- ¾ pound parsnips (or about 5 small parsnips), peeled and coarsely chopped
- 1 large sweet potato peeled and coarsely chopped
- 1 small head of cauliflower coarsely chopped
- ½ cup chicken broth (low-sodium)
- ½ cup water
- Himalayan Pink Salt
- Freshly ground pepper
- Minced chives (optional)

Start by roasting a head of garlic.

Melt three tablespoons of butter in a large stock pot or Dutch oven over medium heat and sauté the onions until translucent (about 5 minutes).

While the onions cook, prep your parsnips, sweet potato, and cauliflower. Add the chopped veggies into the pot, and now the roasted garlic.

Sprinkle some salt, add the broth and water to the pot and bring to a boil. Then, lower the heat to a simmer, cover the pot, and cook for 25–30 minutes or until the vegetables can be easily pierced by a fork.

Season to taste with salt and pepper.

Purée the mixture with an immersion blender or a food processor until smooth. Top with fresh chives and serve!

Makes 4 servings.

Per serving: 224 Calories; 7 g Protein; 32 g Carbohydrate; 10 g Sugar (from the parsnip); 9.5 g Fat

Herb Tuna Salad

- 1 can tuna, in water
- 1 tablespoon chia seeds
- 1 large vine-ripened tomato, cut into wedges
- 1 cucumber, diced
- ½ of a red onion, sliced
- 1–2 stalks celery

Makes 2 servings.

Per serving: 129 Calories; 18 g Protein; 13 g Carbohydrate; 7 g Sugar; 2 g Fat

Dressing:

- ¼ cup olive oil
- 2 tablespoons freshly-squeezed lemon juice
- 1–2 tablespoons fresh parsley (chopped) or fresh dill (to taste)
- 1 large garlic clove, minced
- 1 teaspoon Dijon mustard
- ¼ teaspoon salt
- Ground black pepper to taste

Whisk together dressing ingredients.

Mix all salad ingredients in a large bowl. Toss with dressing. Season with pepper and extra salt, if desired.

Makes 2 servings.

Per serving: 238 Calories; 0 g Protein; 0 g Carbohydrate; 0 g Sugar; 27 g Fat

Immune-Boosting Chocolate-Cherry Green Smoothie

- 8 ounces vanilla unsweetened almond milk
- ½ cup frozen cherries, pitted
- 2 tablespoons chia seeds
- 1 teaspoon vanilla
- 1 tablespoon cacao powder
- 3 cups baby spinach

Blend all ingredients.

Makes 1 serving.

Per serving: 250 Calories; 12 g Protein; 9 g Sugar; 9 g Fat

WHY THE CHERRY?

Cherry Nutrition and Health Benefits

Cherries provide a powerful dose of antioxidants and are considered a "superfruit." Cherries contain beta carotene, vitamin C, potassium, magnesium, iron, folate, and fiber. Tart or sour cherries contain more beta carotene and slightly more vitamin C.

Anthocyanins are antioxidants that give the cherry its red color. It is this antioxidant that has anti-inflammatory properties and can help with symptoms of arthritis. Eating cherries may help reduce the risk of heart disease and certain cancers (breast and colon).

Cherries are low on the glycemic chart and are a great choice for those watching their sugar intake. Cherries are among a few foods that contain melatonin. Melatonin is a natural hormone that helps regulate your body's sleep patterns, and studies show that it may also play a role in preventing memory loss. So, cap your night off with this smoothie knowing you've been kind to yourself all day.

Chicken with Apple and Sage

- 4 chicken breasts, cleaned and pounded slightly with a mallet (to break up fibers and make it moist) Cut each breast in half across the grain (not tip to tip but across the middle) and season with salt and pepper.
- 1 apple cut in ¼- to ½-inch slices
- Fresh sage (~10 leaves, ripped)
- Coconut oil spray
- ¼ cup chicken broth
- ¼ cup marsala wine or OJ

Place chicken in bag with broth, wine, and/or OJ. Add 5 ripped leaves of sage and let marinate.

Heat pan to medium-low, spray with Coconut and pour chicken in with contents of bag in one layer. Cook covered for about 5 minutes on one side. Flip chicken and add apples and rest of sage. Cover and cook until chicken is done, about 6–7 more minutes (maybe 10).

The sauce looks like water, but the chicken has a nice flavor.

Makes 4 servings.

Per serving: 201 Calories; 28 g Protein; 7 g Carbohydrate; 4 g Sugar; 6 g Fat

CHAPTER 9

Week 4

Weight this week:

What were your takeaways this week?

Are there any challenges you are still facing? Remember go deep and be honest with yourself. GO DEEP!

This is your PIVOTal point. This is where your true change is going to happen. This is where new habits begin to stick. Remember it's not magic, everyone. This is where your new mindset and lack of excuses lead you to success.

Friendly Reminders:

Remember sugar is the enemy: Your main meals and mini-meals should be protein, veggie and good fat–based. These three are key to keeping your metabolism high, your cells clean, and your body working properly.

Portion Control: Proteins and carbs should not be larger than your fist.

Healthy Fats Daily: One half to a full avocado, one to three tablespoons oils, handful of nuts (about ten), one to three tablespoons nut butter, etc.

At this point of the challenge you should have found your GO-TO FOODS, your favorites, and what works for you and are safe.

CLEAN CUT TIP

Remember to grab a pretty basket for your kitchen counter and put your newly discovered recipes in it so when you are looking for something fun and new to try, you have them in reach!

If you choose, you can continue to add a few approved complex carbohydrates to your plan this week. We want you to focus on how your body is reacting to foods. Taking notes and using MyFitnessPal are great tools to help keep taking the weight off and from putting it back on. Are you stuck? Visit our site for tips on how to bust through plateaus.

Remember, you have a goal! It may not be met in 6 weeks, but this program is designed to be your foundation for life, not a quick fix. Take it step by step...you can do this!!! PLEASE note how you felt last week adding them in. We can't emphasize enough that these are good for you but if they are overused or trigger you, then you need to pull back!!!

Education

GMO, what is it? Genetically Modified Organism

Food is not made the same as it was years ago. Our environment has changed, the population has increased, more farmers and companies process food, etc., and this has all led to manufacturers manipulating how they increase production of products that come to market. The foods have changed, but the way our bodies process food has not.

When we ingest these genetically modified foods, they are foreign to our system and cannot be broken down as a source of energy, vitamins, minerals, etc. So, what happens to it? It turns to FAT or makes us more susceptible to diseases.

Four Tips to Help Eat GMO-Free:

GMO: Living organisms whose genetic material has been artificially manipulated in a laboratory through genetic engineering. This creates combinations of plant, animal, bacteria, and virus genes that do not occur in nature or through traditional crossbreeding methods. We can talk about this for hours, but we will leave you with this. One of the ways to decrease having to spray crops with pesticide is to genetically modify them with pesticides. Cross pollination spreads this. Animals eating the GMO crops are now infected. These highly toxic chemicals have also been linked to cancer.

1. Buy organic: They cannot include GMO ingredients if they are certified organic.

2. Look for "Non-GMO Project" seals on food (see seal on app above).

3. Avoid at-risk ingredients such as soybeans, canola, corn, and sugar from sugar beets.

4. Buy from the list provided on this link: http://responsibletechnology.org/nongmoshoppingguide.pdf?key=28876010

To help guide you through these types of foods, here are a few tips and links, and an app to help go GMO-free.

APP: The Non-GMO Project App will help you choose non-GMO foods while shopping in the App Store. It's called Non-GMO project shopping guide.

LINK TO THE APP:

http://livingnongmo.org/learn/about/?utm_source=google&utm_medium=cpc&gclid=CjoKCQiAuf7fBRD7ARIsACqb8w7v1VVp1TFcmn7yAT4-33TACRTfBUj0El1TkTBdLoiavGZEa4q7psUaAgtaEALw_wcB

Your Organic Food List

A list is put out every year by the Environmental Working Group (EWG) about what foods contain the most pesticide residue. The Dirty Dozen is the list you really should be using to buy organic. The clean 15 are the fruits and vegetables that

> ORGANIC: Organic crops cannot be grown with synthetic fertilizers, synthetic pesticides or sewage sludge (SLUDGE?! GROSS!). They cannot be genetically engineered or irradiated.

had the least pesticide residue when tested. Their website is www.ewg.org. They also provide amazing info on GMO, sunscreen, makeup, and more.

Download EWG's Healthy Living App Today!

Ratings for more than 120,000 food and personal care products, now at your fingertips.

> Animals must eat only organically-grown feed (without animal byproducts) and can't be treated with synthetic hormones or antibiotics. They must have access to the outdoors, and ruminants (hoofed animals, including cows) must have access to pasture. They also cannot be cloned.

DIRTY DOZEN (2019) UPDATE

1. Strawberries
2. Spinach
3. Kale
4. Nectarines
5. Apples
6. Grapes
7. Peaches
8. Cherries
9. Pears
10. Tomatoes
11. Celery
12. Potatoes

CLEAN FIFTEEN (2019)

1. Avocados
2. Sweet Corn*
3. Pineapples
4. Sweet Peas (frozen)
5. Onions
6. Papayas*
7. Eggplants
8. Asparagus
9. Kiwis
10. Cabbages
11. Cauliflower
12. Cantaloupes
13. Broccoli
14. Mushrooms
15. Honeydew Melons

*A small amount of sweet corn, papaya and summer squash sold in the United States is produced from genetically modified seeds. Buy organic varieties of these crops if you want to avoid genetically modified produce.

Source: www.ewg.org

Week 4 Menu Guide

Day 1		
Breakfast	**Lunch**	**Dinner**
Quinoa Chia Spiced Breakfast Bowl (see recipes)	4 ounces protein (like turkey, chicken or tuna salad) over greens (unlimited greens and veggies) 2 teaspoons of olive oil with lemon, Pink Himalayan salt, and pepper on your veggies **OR** Your "GO-TO"	Salmon with Roasted Brussels Sprouts (see recipes)
Snack	**Snack**	**Snack**
Cucumber dipped in mashed avocado (add garlic powder, red pepper, etc.)	Shake **OR** Your "go-to" at this point	Clean Popcorn (see recipes)

Day 2

Breakfast	Lunch	Dinner
Your favorite egg quiche or eggs any way, on sprouted toast	Turkey roll-ups with roasted red pepper over leftover veggies from dinner	Savory Mushroom Meatballs (see recipes) with any side veggie
Snack	**Snack**	**Snack**
¼ cup berries or ½ a green apple with a ½ handful of nuts or 1 teaspoon of nut butter (or what has been working for you)	¼–½ cup edamame with cherry tomatoes or ½ cup of breakfast quinoa bowl	Handful of nuts

Day 3

Breakfast	Lunch	Dinner
Greek yogurt with cinnamon or a slice of approved homemade Pumpkin Bread (see recipes) with a teaspoon of Irish butter (Tip, cut half the loaf and freeze it so you don't pick at it all day.)	Leftover meatballs (3–4) with greens	Shrimp and Avocado Salad (see recipes) or any grilled protein with side of asparagus almond salad
Snack	**Snack**	**Snack**
½ an apple with rolled turkey (3 slices) or 1 teaspoon of nut butter	½ sliced avocado with pink salt/ pepper and 1 hard-boiled egg	2 teaspoons nut butter

Day 4		
Breakfast	**Lunch**	**Dinner**
2 hard-boiled eggs ¼ of an avocado	4 ounces protein like turkey, chicken, tuna salad, etc. over greens with veggies 2 teaspoons of olive oil, with lemon juice, pink sea salt, and pepper, **OR** Use veggies from Wednesday night with tuna salad wrapped in a coconut wrap.	Shallot Shrimp (see recipes) with Coconut Cinnamon Sweet Potatoes (see recipes)
Snack	**Snack**	**Snack**
½ Greek yogurt with berries and 5 crushed nuts	1 teaspoon of nut butter or 1 full egg with hummus and hot sauce	Clean popcorn

Day 5		
Breakfast	**Lunch**	**Dinner**
Shake or eggs any way you like, or a slice of approved homemade pumpkin bread with a teaspoon of Irish butter	Leftover sweet potato (½ cup) with 4 oz of organic rotisserie chicken	Shredded chicken (from a fully cooked organic chicken) over a big Kale Salad (see recipes) or roasted veggies Salsa ½ avocado
Snack	**Snack**	**Snack**
½ apple, sliced, wrapped in 4 slices of turkey dipped in honey mustard or ½ serving of pumpkin chia pudding	Nuts	½ serving of chia pudding

Day 6		
Breakfast	**Lunch**	**Dinner**
½ cup pumpkin chia pudding with 1 teaspoon of nut butter	Nice salad with spicy chicken or chicken salad, olive oil, lemon/lime, salt, and pepper with honey mustard	Spicy white chili
Snack	**Snack**	**Snack**
Cucumber with salt and little walnut oil, with ½ an avocado	2 teaspoons nut butter	1 slice of pumpkin bread

Day 7		
Breakfast	**Lunch**	**Dinner**
2 eggs anyway you like them with hot sauce and ½ avocado, or quinoa breakfast bowl	Leftover chili	Spiralized zucchini noodles with shrimp
Snack	**Snack**	**Snack**
½ Greek yogurt with drizzle of honey and berries	1–2 hard-boiled eggs with cucumber, salt/pepper, and walnut oil (Love this snack!)	½ cup quinoa breakfast or ½ cup chia pudding or 2 pieces of dark chocolate or 1 slice pumpkin bread

Recipes

Quinoa Chia Spiced Breakfast Bowl

- 1 cup cooked quinoa
  - o Quinoa Tip: You can use a pre-cooked quinoa. Or make quinoa the night before. (Note: You need to soak raw quinoa for about 15 minutes before cooking. For fluffy quinoa, we use ¼–½ cup less water than on the directions.)
- 1 large egg white plus ¼ cup unsweetened almond or coconut milk
- 1 tablespoon raw honey
- ½ teaspoon pure vanilla extract
- ½-1 teaspoon pumpkin spice, or the following:
- ¼ teaspoon ground cinnamon
- ¼ teaspoon ground ginger (optional)
- ¼ teaspoon nutmeg
- Unsweetened coconut flakes and/or nuts for topping (optional)

Instructions:

Reheat cooked quinoa in saucepan; remove from stove and stir in egg white, vanilla, milk, and spices.

Return pan to stove, covering again with a tiny crack for steam to escape, and continue to cook on low until almost all the milk has been absorbed, about 5 minutes. Top with coconut or nuts.

Makes 2 servings.

Per serving: 158 Calories: 4 g Protein; 19.5 g Carbohydrate; 1 g Sugar; 2 g Fat

With 1 tablespoon coconut flakes and 1 tablespoon almond slivers:

Per serving: 188.5 Calories: 5 g Protein; 21 g Carbohydrate; 1 g Sugar; 5 g Fat

Pumpkin Chia Pudding

- 1½ cups coconut milk or unsweetened almond milk
- ¾ cup pumpkin puree
- ½ teaspoon vanilla extract
- ½ teaspoon cinnamon
- ¼ teaspoon allspice or pumpkin spice
- ¼ cup chia seeds

Mix it all in a plastic container and chill.

Makes 2 servings.

Per serving: 182.5 Calories: 7.5 g Protein; 18 g Carbohydrate; 3 g Sugar; 9 g Fat

Pumpkin Bread

- 2 cup Paleo flour (like Bob's Red Mill)
- ¼ teaspoon pink salt
- 1 teaspoon baking soda
- ½ tablespoon cinnamon
- ½ teaspoon pumpkin or apple pie spice
- 1 can (15-ounce) pumpkin puree

- 2 teaspoons vanilla
- 2 tablespoons honey
- 3 whole eggs
- ¼ of a bag of chocolate chips (about ¼ cup)

With an electric mixer combine pumpkin, honey, eggs, and vanilla until all combined. Then add the flour, salt, baking soda, spices, and chocolate chips, and mix until just combined.

Spray a small loaf pan (8.4 x 4.5) with coconut oil spray and scoop batter into pan. Bake at 350° F for 50–60 minutes. Cool for 1 hour.

Makes 4 servings.

Per serving: 215 Calories; 11 g Protein; 21 g Carbohydrate; 6 g Sugar; 8 g Fat

Coconut-Cinnamon Sweet Potatoes

- 5 medium sweet potatoes, peeled and cut into ¾-inch pieces (about 6 cups)
- ¾ cup light coconut milk
- 1 teaspoon cinnamon (more to taste)
- 1 teaspoon pure vanilla extract
- ½ teaspoon Pink Himalayan salt
- ⅛ teaspoon fresh ground black pepper
- ⅛ teaspoon cayenne pepper
- ½ cup unsalted pecan halves, chopped

Preheat oven to 325° F. Bring a large pot of water to a boil over high heat. Add sweet potatoes, return to boiling and cook until soft, about 10 minutes. Drain and transfer potatoes to the bowl of a stand mixer (or use a large bowl and a hand-held electric mixer).

Add coconut milk, cinnamon, vanilla, salt, black pepper, and cayenne to potatoes. Mix on medium speed until smooth, scraping down sides of bowl once or twice. Transfer to a 9 x 9-inch baking dish. Sprinkle pecans evenly over sweet potato mixture.

Bake 45 to 50 minutes, or until edges are slightly browned. Cool on a rack for 10 minutes and serve.

One cup is a serving. This recipe serves 6.

Per serving: 158 Calories; 2.5 g Protein; 28 g Carbohydrate; 6.1 g Sugar; 4.8 g Fat

Spicy White Chili

- 1 ½ pounds chicken breast, cubed or shredded
- 2 medium onions, chopped
- 1 tablespoon oil
- 4 garlic cloves, minced
- 2 cans (4-ounce) chopped green chilies
- 2 teaspoons ground cumin
- 1 teaspoon dried oregano
- ¼ teaspoon cayenne pepper
- ¼ teaspoon ground cloves
- 28 oz low-sodium chicken broth
- 3 cans great northern beans, rinsed and drained

In a 3-quart saucepan, sauté onions in oil until tender. Stir in garlic, chili, cumin, oregano, cayenne, and cloves; cook and stir 2–3 minutes more.

Add broth, chicken, and beans; simmer, uncovered, for 15 minutes. Remove from heat.

Garnish sliced jalapeño peppers, if desired.

Makes 6 servings.

Per serving: 365 Calories; 29.5 g Protein; 14.5 g Carbohydrate; 2 g Sugar; 7 g Fat

Basic Kale Salad

- 1 bunch of kale, stems removed, rinsed and patted dry
- ½ cup unsweetened dried cranberries
- Juice of one lemon
- 1 tablespoon of olive oil
- 1 teaspoon local honey
- ¼ cup almond slices
- Salt and pepper to taste
- 2 teaspoons grated raw parmesan cheese

Chop kale into small pieces. Add a small dose of olive oil and massage the kale. This breaks down the fibers and brings out flavor. It also softens it.

To make dressing, stir lemon juice, olive oil, honey, salt, and pepper together in a large bowl.

Add chopped kale, cranberries, almond slices, and parmesan to bowl with dressing.

Stir all ingredients together and serve.

KALE SALAD TIP

Massaging the kale prior to adding the other ingredients, or with the dressing is key with kale. It will soften it, bring more flavor, and taste amazing!

Makes 2 servings.

Per serving: 263 Calories; 9 g Protein; 22 g Carbohydrate; 5.5 g Sugar; 17 g Fat

Savory Mushroom Meatballs

- 8 medium, fresh shiitake mushrooms or any mushroom of choice, minced
- 1 medium shallot, minced
- 2 tablespoons minced cilantro or basil
- 2 pounds ground chicken
- 2 tablespoons tomato paste
- Pink salt
- Freshly-ground black pepper

Line two rimmed baking sheets with parchment paper or foil and place a cooling rack on top of each. Preheat the oven to 375° F.

In a large bowl, combine the ground meat, tomato paste, minced veggies, and herbs. Sprinkle with pink salt (generously) and pepper. Thoroughly combine the ingredients but don't overwork the meat.

Roll out three dozen meatballs. Each meatball should be about the size of golf ball. Divide the meatballs onto the two lined baking sheets. Bake each tray of meatballs for 15 to 20 minutes, flipping the meatballs at the halfway mark.

You can also freeze the cooked meatballs for up to 6 months. Four meatballs = one serving.

Makes 9 servings.

Per serving: 177 Calories; 19.1 g Protein; 2.6 g Carbohydrate; 1.6 g Sugar; 10 g Fat

Shrimp and Avocado Salad

- ¼ cup olive oil
- 3 tablespoons lime juice
- 1 garlic clove
- ¾ teaspoon Pink Himalayan salt
- ½ teaspoon ground black pepper
- Greens of your choice (Butter lettuce or spinach works great.)
- 1 pound cooked medium-sized shrimp
- 1 avocado pitted, peeled, and cubed
- 1 pint cherry tomatoes
- ½ cup thinly sliced basil

Whisk together olive oil, lime juice, garlic, salt, and pepper in a large bowl. Remove 2 tablespoons of the lime juice mixture to another large bowl, add lettuce and toss.

Toss shrimp, avocado, tomatoes, and basil with remaining lime juice mixture. Place lettuce on a serving plate and top with shrimp mixture.

Makes 4 servings.

Per serving: 321 Calories; 27.5 g Protein; 8.5 g Carbohydrate; 3 g Sugar; 21 g Fat

Shallot Shrimp

- 1 pound of shrimp, cleaned and peeled
- 2 small shallots, diced, or one big one
- 2 tablespoons of olive oil
- 2 teaspoons clarified butter (ghee or Irish butter)
- ¼ cup white wine

Heat oil in pan to med-high heat, then lower to medium-low and put in shallots; cook them slowly so they don't burn.

Add the shrimp in a single layer. Once one side is pink, flip and add wine, butter, and a little salt. (Shrimp are salty.)

Serve! This recipe is so easy and healthy!

SHRIMP TIP!

If you buy frozen shrimp, place them in cold water for about 10 minutes before you're ready to cook, and they will thaw.

Makes 4 servings.

Per serving: 220 Calories; 25.5 g Protein; 13.2 g Carbohydrate; 3 g Sugar; 45g Fat

Salmon and Roasted Brussels Sprouts

FOR THE BRUSSELS SPROUTS

- 1 pound Brussels sprouts, trimmed
- 1.5 tablespoons olive oil
- 1 clove of garlic, chopped
- ½ onion chopped
- Dash of pink salt

FOR THE SALMON

- Salmon fillet (4–5 ounces), skinned
- 1 tablespoon olive oil
- 3 to 4 garlic cloves, minced
- 1 tablespoon dried oregano
- ½ teaspoon salt
- Fresh ground pepper, to taste
- ¼ teaspoon fresh ground pepper

Preheat oven to 450° F. Lightly grease a rimmed baking sheet with cooking spray or line with parchment paper and set aside.

In a large mixing bowl combine trimmed Brussels sprouts, olive oil, garlic, salt, and pepper; mix until well combined.

Transfer Brussels sprouts to previously prepared baking sheet; arrange in a single layer and bake for 15 minutes, stirring once or twice during cooking.

In the meantime, prepare the salmon.

Drizzle salmon with olive oil.

Evenly divide and press minced garlic on top of each fillet.

Season with oregano, salt, and pepper.

Remove baking sheet from oven; add the onion and mix with the Brussels sprouts, then move them around making empty spots for the salmon fillets.

Place salmon in the empty spots and bake for 10 to 12 minutes, or until salmon is cooked through.

Remove from oven; let stand 2 minutes and serve.

Per serving: 368 Calories; 30 g Protein; 26.5 g Carbohydrate; 6 g Sugar; 19 g Fat

Homemade Clean Cut Popcorn

- ¼ cup organic popcorn kernels
- 1 brown paper bag
- 1 teaspoon butter, melted (optional)
- Spices of your choice

In a brown paper bag, add ¼ cup organic popcorn kernels and pop in microwave until kernels are popped. Every microwave is different. I go about 2 minutes at a time and watch it.

When popped, add a little melted butter (optional) with spices of your choice!

Makes 1 serving.

Per serving: 140 Calories; 17 g Carbohydrate; 8 g Fat

CHAPTER 10

Week 5

Weight This Week:

What were your takeaways this week?

Any Setbacks?

Think about what's getting easier and what is still challenging you. GO DEEP!

IT'S TIME TO TAKE CHARGE THIS WEEK!

Clean Cut Recharge

Here is your recharge plan. These tools can be used if you have a bad day or hit a plateau.

- Intermittent fasting: (See the natural remedies in chapter 4).
- You can always go back to week one for a few days; this means no complex carbs, no fruit and no cheats or treats to help you reset, refocus and confuse your body again.

OR...you will love this one. If you haven't had a cheat, do it. Have a big cheat. It's time. For example, enjoy a bowl of pasta or a slice of pizza or some extra quinoa at dinner. Don't go completely off the reservation, but sometimes that cheat tricks your body, so when you go back to the Clean Cut way, your body reacts again, and you begin to lose.

- Adding an extra day of exercise is always another way to change it up.

If you choose to go back to week one, do it from Monday to Wednesday or Thursday. This means no sugar at all, not even fruit, and no complex carbs. If you haven't added them back at this point, try intermittent fasting or have that one big cheat.

You should be seeing results and changes in your body, but if you have fallen off a bit or hit that plateau, use the tips above. This is a good week to check back in with yourself, be honest. Take notice and see where maybe some old habits are coming back or maybe you aren't watching your portions as much. Just become mindful again!

Remember everyone's body works a little differently, and this is not an exact science. This is why a food journal is so helpful. Some people are super clean and see no results for a few days, and then suddenly they are down 2 pounds. Watch for your cycles; see how it happens for you. At this point, if you've been following the program, you may have noticed your pattern.

PRE-PLAN

This seems to be the top culprit. You MUST PRE-PLAN. Life is stressful.

THIS WEEK, really focus on pre-planning. Remember PREP is KEY! You have all the tools; now they just need to be put back into play and become a real PIVOT in life.

- It is time to go back, look, and give yourself credit for all the changes you have made this month. Go through the recipes, pick out your favorites and use them again. You don't need to reinvent things

If it's working, stay with it. Separate out snacks, breakfast, lunch, and dinners so if you have a brain freeze or are just planning, you can easily get to them and plan your day, days or week!

Play with recipes and make them your own. You have the tools now to add healthy ingredients and make SMART decisions.

CLEAN CUT TIP

Create grocery store lists of your FAVE foods, so you can have a staple list. Put it in the NOTES section of your phone to have it with you in case you forget!

Week 5 Menu Guide

Day 1		
Breakfast	**Lunch**	**Dinner**
Egg cups with ½ an avocado	6 ounces turkey lunch meat wrapped around peppers and cucumbers with hot sauce or any lunch you've been enjoying without the carb or fruit	Chickpea and Butternut Squash stew (see recipes)
Snack	**Snack**	**Snack**
5 raw mushroom caps stuffed with Clean Cut tuna	Protein shake (no fruit, can add 1 teaspoon of nut butter)	Nuts or nut butter

Day 2		
Breakfast	**Lunch**	**Dinner**
Veggie omelette (load it up with veggies!) or one of the quiches	Chicken or tuna salad wrapped in a leafy green or coconut wrap, with smashed avocado	6 ounces Ginger Shrimp (see recipes) Big salad or roasted veggies or a cauliflower rice from past weeks
Snack	**Snack**	**Snack**
½ Edamame Cucumber alad (see recipe) with scoop of tuna salad	1 cup chopped veggies Mashed avocado with lime, pink salt, and pepper	nuts or nut butter or 2 hard-boiled eggs and cherry tomatoes

Day 3

Breakfast	Lunch	Dinner
Green Juice	Leftover roasted veggies with 5 slices of turkey or tuna salad	Slow Cooker Shredded Chicken (see recipes)
Snack	**Snack**	**Snack**
2 hard-boiled eggs, salt, and pepper	½ avocado with salt, pepper, and cherry tomatoes	Nuts (Add a piece of dark chocolate for a yummy treat!)

Day 4

Breakfast	Lunch	Dinner
A slice of sprouted bread and avocado mash drizzled with hot sauce or everything bagel seasoning	Leftover slow roast chicken with any veggie you like	Fish Tacos (see recipes)
Snack	**Snack**	**Snack**
10 nuts or 2 hard-boiled eggs or a combo	Any protein snack you've been using or veggies unlimited	Nut butter or nuts

Day 5		
Breakfast	**Lunch**	**Dinner**
Slice of sprouted bread with one fried egg, tomato, and hot sauce	Edamame salad with tuna fish	Cauliflower soup (see recipes)
Snack	**Snack**	**Snack**
½ apple with 1 teaspoon nut butter	Shake with ¼ cup berries, greens of choice	Any protein or veggies

Day 6		
Breakfast	**Lunch**	**Dinner**
Eggs any way with veggies	Leftover cauliflower oup	Chicken and Sweet Potato Crock Pot (see recipes)
Snack	**Snack**	**Snack**
Nuts or 1 teaspoon nut butter	Veggies or shake with 1 teaspoon nut butter	2 hard-boiled eggs with hot sauce

Day 7		
Breakfast	**Lunch**	**Dinner**
Shake with ¼ cup berries, chia seeds and any greens you like	Leftover chicken and sweet potato from crock pot	Seared 4-ounce filet mignon with roasted Brussels sprouts, sliced mushrooms, lots of pepper, salt, and olive oil (YUM)
Snack	**Snack**	**Snack**
2 hard-boiled eggs with ½ an avocado	Nuts	2 squares of good dark chocolate

Clean Cut Slow Cooker Shredded Chicken and Salsa Sauce

You can use the salsa verde recipe here (below), or if you want a quick throw in the crock pot and go, grab some deli container fresh Pico de Gallo or salsa verde.

For Chicken:

- 2 pounds chicken breast
- 4 teaspoons minced garlic
- 1 teaspoon cumin
- 1 teaspoon pink sea salt
- 1–2 tablespoons chopped chipotle peppers in adobo sauce (depends on the kick you want)
- Black pepper to taste

Add chicken to slow cooker with garlic, cumin, salt, chipotle pepper, and black pepper with 1 cup of the salsa mixture. Mix up and set for 4 hours on high or 7 hours on low.

Cover and refrigerate the remaining salsa sauce.

When chicken is done, shred, then add remaining salsa. Warm in crock pot and serve!

Makes 6 servings.

Per serving: 172 Calories: 34 g Protein; 1.2 g Carbohydrate; 0 g Sugar; 1.7 g Fat

To Make Your Own Salsa Verde Sauce:

- 7 tomatillos
- 1 poblano pepper

- 1 shallot
- ½ cup cilantro
- 2–4 large garlic cloves
- 1 teaspoon pink sea salt
- 1 tablespoon olive oil

Line a baking sheet with the tomatillos and poblano pepper. Broil about 6 inches from heat, turning once until softened and slightly charred. This should take about 8–10 minutes.

*FUN TIP! Put the poblano pepper in a heat proof bowl and cover with plastic wrap. Let it sit for 10–15 minutes and then peel the skins off and cut peppers up into small pieces.

Transfer the tomatillos to a blender. Add the shallot, cilantro, garlic and salt. Blend up until smooth. Add the poblano pepper and blend until combined.

In a pan, heat the oil, then add the mixture and bring to a simmer. Stir frequently for about 5 minutes. Remove and let cool.

Makes 4 servings.

Per serving: 67 Calories; 0.5 g Protein; 7.75 g Carbohydrate; 3 g Sugar; 3.5 g Fat

Edamame and Cucumber Salad

- 2 cups edamame, frozen
- 1–2 cucumbers
- 1 teaspoon garlic, fresh
- 1 jalapeño pepper
- 1 red bell pepper, large

Dressing

- 1 ½ teaspoons Dijon mustard
- 2 teaspoons ginger paste or fresh ginger
- 1 tablespoon olive oil
- 1 tablespoon apple cider vinegar
- Squeeze of lemon or lime
- 1 teaspoon red pepper flakes
- 1 teaspoon sesame seeds

Combine dressing ingredients and whisk, then add to edamame and cucumbers.

Makes 2 servings.

Per serving: 307 Calories; 17 g Protein; 24 g Carbohydrate; 4.5g Sugar; 13 g Fat

Clean Cut Flavorful Cauliflower Soup

- 1 tablespoon Irish butter
- 1 teaspoon arrowroot or cornstarch
- 1 medium head cauliflower
- ½ cup chopped shallots
- 2 cloves chopped garlic
- 2–3 sprigs rosemary
- ¼ teaspoon cinnamon
- 4 cups low-sodium chicken or veggie broth
- Salt and pepper to taste

In a medium saucepan, make a roux by melting the butter on low heat. Add the arrowroot and stir about 2 minutes.

Add the chicken broth, onions, and cauliflower, and set heat to medium. Bring to a boil, then cover and simmer over medium-low heat until vegetables are tender (about 20 minutes.)

Puree with an immersion blender until smooth. Season with salt and pepper.

CLEAN CUT TIP

Sometimes the cornstarch or arrowroot clumps when you add it. For a smooth roux, you can add a little water to make a paste before you add to the butter.

Makes 2 servings.

Per serving: 271 Calories; 19 g Protein; 26.5 g Carbohydrate; 11 g Sugar; 6g Fat

Clean Cut Fish Tacos and Cabbage Slaw

You can use this slaw as a side or as a topping for other meals and you can use a whitefish of choice like tilapia, cod or halibut.

Slaw

- 1 bag of raw slaw veggies (bagged) (green cabbage, red cabbage, and carrots)
- ½–1 bunch of chopped cilantro
- 1 lime, squeezed
- 1–2 cloves of garlic, to taste
- 1 tomato, chopped
- ½ onion, chopped
- 1 tablespoon olive oil
- 1 tablespoon apple cider vinegar
- 1 tablespoon Greek yogurt
- Jalapeño, chopped (totally optional)

Fish Marinade

- 1 tablespoon olive oil
- 1 teaspoon cumin
- 1 tablespoon chili powder
- 1 clove garlic
- 1 small lime, juiced
- Cayenne to taste

Mix all ingredients for slaw and set aside to marinade and take on the flavor. Mix up marinade seasoning and place in a Ziploc bag with fish. Marinate 20 minutes. Preheat oven to 400° F and bake fish for 15 minutes or until fish flakes easily with a fork.

You can use coconut wraps or lettuce wraps to enjoy your tacos.

Makes 4 servings.

Per serving: 222 Calories; 31 g Protein; 4.75 g Carbohydrate; 2.55 g Sugar; 7.75 g Fat

With 1 coconut wrap:

Per serving: Calories: 292, Protein; 20g, Carbohydrate; 5g, Sugar; 14g, Fat

Easy Chicken and Sweet Potato Crock Pot

- 2 chicken breasts, cut into 1-inch pieces
- 2 sweet potatoes, peeled and cubed
- ½ box low-sodium chicken broth (14.5 ounces)
- 1 teaspoon pink salt
- 1–2 cloves garlic
- 1 tablespoon thyme
- 1½ teaspoons black pepper
- 1 tablespoon minced onion

Put everything in the crock pot. Place lid on top and cook on low for 8 hours. Serve with a side salad or steamed veggies.

Makes 2 servings.

Per serving: 293 Calories; 32 g Protein; 29 g Carbohydrate; 6 g Sugar; 1g Fat

Ginger Shrimp

- 1 bag of raw frozen cleaned shrimp (thawed)
- Fresh ginger, peeled, about 2 inches long
- 1 lime, squeezed
- 1 clove of garlic, to taste
- ½ onion, chopped
- 1 tablespoon olive oil
- 1 tablespoon red wine vinegar
- ¼ teaspoon ground cayenne pepper
- 1 tablespoon chopped cilantro
- Jalapeño, chopped

Chop ginger, garlic, and onion.

Place in large bowl; add salt and pepper to taste; add shrimp, lime, red wine vinegar, and cayenne.

Mix and let sit for 5–10 minutes. Heat skillet, add olive oil and place shrimp and mixture in the pan in one even layer.

Cook shrimp on one side for about 3–4 minutes then turn.

Add the cilantro and jalapeño and cook for another 3–4 minutes.

Serve with veggie of your choice.

Makes 4 servings.

Per serving: 162 Calories; 25.5 g Protein; 2.5 g Carbohydrate; 1 g Sugar; 5.5 g Fat

Chickpea and Butternut Squash Stew

- 1 medium butternut squash, cut into 1½-inch chunks (about 6 cups)
- 3 tablespoons extra-virgin olive oil, divided
- Himalayan Pink Salt to taste
- Ground black pepper to taste
- 2 medium onions, chopped
- 8 large cloves garlic, finely chopped
- ¼ cup finely chopped cilantro
- 1½ teaspoons ground cumin
- 1 teaspoon paprika
- 1½ cups vegetable broth
- 2 cups of greens of your choice
- 3 medium carrots, cut into ¾-inch cubes
- 2 cans (15.5-ounce) chickpeas, rinsed and drained
- 1 can (28-ounce) diced, fire-roasted tomatoes
- 4 teaspoons harissa sauce

Preheat oven to 375° F. Toss squash with 1 ½ tablespoons olive oil, salt and pepper. Spray a baking sheet and lay squash in a single layer. Roast for 40–45 minutes.

In a large skillet, add remaining 1½ tablespoons olive oil and heat on medium-high. Add onions and salt and pepper to taste. Cook for 3 to 4 minutes. Stir in garlic and cook for another 3 minutes.

Stir in cilantro, cumin, and paprika, and cook for 1 minute. Add carrots and 1 cup of vegetable broth to the mixture. Bring to a boil over high heat. Reduce heat to low and simmer, covered, until carrots are tender, 10 to 12 minutes.

Add tomatoes, greens, and chickpeas. Raise heat to medium-high and simmer for 10 minutes. Stir in harissa paste, roasted squash, and remaining ½ cup veggie broth.

Simmer uncovered for another 3–5 minutes.

Makes 8 servings.

Per serving: 236 Calories: 8 g Protein; 40 g Carbohydrate; 8.25 g Sugar; 6.25 g Fat

CHAPTER 11

Week 6

Weight this week?

What was your biggest takeaway this week?

Have you been able to put it all together?

If not, what do you want to continue to work on?

Bring it all together here. Write your 6-week story and where you are headed for success!

DOCUMENT YOUR THOUGHTS AND
HOLD YOURSELF ACCOUNTABLE

Download a printable version at www.cleancutfit.com/bookclub

- WHAT ARE YOU GOING TO DO TO CONTINUE YOUR LIFESTYLE CHANGE?
- WHAT WORKS FOR YOU?

- WHAT ARE YOUR GO-TO MEALS/SNACKS/FOODS?
- WHAT ARE YOU STILL STRUGGLING WITH?
- WHAT WAS A BIG AH-HA MOMENT FOR YOU?
- WHAT IS YOUR MANTRA?

Putting It All Together

You have done the work, and now it's time to continue your journey or maintain. You have learned to manage your cravings, eat out, curb your food around your cheats, and use the natural tips and tricks that make balance possible. Take all you've learned with you and apply it each day. Clean food is not a punishment; it's being kind to yourself. We are always running virtual challenges so please check in because we truly are always here.

Welcome to the Clean Cut Family.

The tools you've used aren't just for these six weeks. This is a REAL LIFESTYLE. This is how you will ultimately live life. Monday–Thursday, CLEAN. Friday, enjoy a treat. Weekends, have a cheat and work around it. MOVE, MINDFULNESS, PREP, HONEST, NO EXCUSES, AND OWN IT! We will all slip, but don't fall. Get right back up. Don't beat yourself up over it. You've learned what to do, and now you just have to DO IT!

This journal page is for you. It is here to help you continue your journey to your goals. This is not over, it's just the beginning. Summarize your struggles, accomplishments and goals from the past six weeks. Use this to look back and keep going. These questions are here for you to help you through the tough times and be proud of what you have accomplished! We will always be here for you and are so proud to be part of this journey.

Welcome to your NEW LIFESTYLE!

_____

_____

_____

_____

_____

_____

_____

_____

_____

_____

SUMMARY OF SUCCESS

- ACCOUNTABILITY
- Water (with Himalayan Pink Salt)
- Lean protein, veggies, and healthy fats in all meals
- Limit carbs and fruits.
- NO PROCESSED FOODS
- PREPARATION is key.
- Recipe binder/basket (Clean Cut Download will be coming in the future.)
- Trying new recipes and meals, becoming creative, and trying new activities

- Get the family involved.
- GREEN, GREEN, AND MORE GREEN; UNLIMITED Veggies
- NON-GMO
- ORGANIC WHEN YOU CAN (Remember the dirty dozen and work from there.)
- Find foods that satisfy you and go with them. ("Go-To Meals," and they will always change)
- BE HONEST and don't make up excuses; there are no shortcuts.

Remember that just because you find a clean recipe online, it doesn't mean it is unlimited portions. Take what you have learned and modify it for your lifestyle and goals.

This is real food. A treat here and there includes black bean chips, gluten-free chocolate bars, etc. These are all treats, not staples. Your staples come out of your refrigerator. If you keep this mindset, you will succeed. If you try to find ways to replace old habits with healthy versions ALL THE TIME, those old habits will return, we promise. However, the more real food you eat, the better you will feel, and this will stick forever.

LISTEN TO YOUR BODY, really listen, and learn what your cravings mean. A lot of your cravings are society-created. Step away and remember your healthier options. Think before you put that "treat" or "cheat" in your mouth.

BALANCE IS KEY. We want you to enjoy the things you love but work for them; enjoy them and let it go….

THIS WEEK CREATE YOUR GO-TO MENU!

Power Seed Quinoa Breakfast Bowl

- ½ cup cooked quinoa
- ¼ cup unsweetened vanilla almond milk
- 2 tablespoons sliced almonds
- 1 tablespoon sunflower seeds
- ¼ cup berries such as black or raspberry
- 1 teaspoon fresh ripped mint
- 1 teaspoon raw honey

Mix the quinoa with the milk and heat through for about 1 minute.

Add the almonds and seeds and mix. Top with berries, mint, and honey.

Makes 1 serving.

Per serving: 290 Calories; 10 g Protein; 35 g Carbohydrate; 9 g Sugar; 14g Fat

Dijon Sweet Potato Chicken

- 2 tablespoons Dijon mustard
- 2 tablespoons chopped fresh thyme
- 2 tablespoons olive oil
- ½ teaspoon fresh pepper
- 2 pounds chicken breast
- 2 medium sweet potatoes, peeled and cut in 1-inch pieces
- 1 large red onion, cut into 1-inch pieces

Place rack in lower third of oven and preheat oven to 450° F.

Mix the mustard, thyme, oil, and pepper. Add salt to taste.

Toss the sweet potato and onion in the mix and spread onto a lined baking sheet (parchment paper or aluminum foil). Place the chicken on top of potatoes. Roast for 30–35 minutes (stirring potatoes halfway through).

Serve with any greens you like.

Makes 6 servings.

Per serving: 254 Calories; 35 g Protein; 11 g Carbohydrate; 3 g Sugar; 6 g Fat

Crock Pot Buffalo Chicken Lettuce Wraps

- 2 pounds boneless, skinless chicken breast (6-8 breasts)
- 1 bottle of Buffalo sauce

Wraps:

- 6 large lettuce leaves, bibb or iceberg
- 2 large celery stalks, cut into 2-inch matchsticks

In a crock-pot, **combine** chicken and buffalo sauce. **Cover** and cook on high 4 hours.

Makes 6 servings.

Per serving: 166 Calories; 34 g Protein; 0 g Carbohydrate; 0 g Sugar; 1.5 g Fat

Basil Chili Stir Fry

- 2 tablespoon olive or coconut oil or Irish Butter (divided)
- 3 red chilies, finely chopped
- 3 garlic cloves, minced
- 2 tablespoons fish sauce, optional (use water if you don't have fish sauce, or do not like it)
- 1 pound of tender lean beef, chicken or shrimp cut in thin slices
- 1 bunch asparagus, chopped
- 1 bell pepper, chopped
- 1 small container sliced mushrooms
- 1 cup fresh basil leaves

Mix the chopped chilies, garlic, and fish sauce in a bowl and add the beef, chicken or shrimp. Put in the refrigerator to marinate for about 2 hours.

Heat the oil or butter in the wok or big pan and stir-fry the protein. When cooked through, remove from the wok/pan.

Add the other tablespoon of oil or butter and stir-fry the veggies. Add ¼ cup water or stock when the veggies are almost cooked (about 5–8 minutes).

Return the beef, chicken or shrimp to the wok, add the basil and cook for another minute.

Garnish the finished dish with slices of chili.

Makes 4 servings.

With Beef: Per serving: 371 Calories; 31 g Protein; 10 g Carbohydrate; 4g Sugar; 22 g Fat

With Chicken: Per serving: 237 Calories; 29 g Protein; 10 g Carbohydrate; 4 g Sugar; 8.25 g Fat

With Shrimp: Per serving: 232 Calories; 29 g Protein; 10 g Carbohydrate; 4 g Sugar; 9 g Fat

Mediterranean Bean Salad

- 1 can (15.5 ounce) garbanzo beans, drained (organic)
- 1 lemon, zested and juiced
- 1 medium tomato, chopped
- ¼ cup chopped red onion
- ½ cup chopped fresh parsley
- 1 teaspoon capers, rinsed and drained
- 3 tablespoons extra virgin olive oil
- ½ teaspoon Pink Himalayan salt, or to taste

In a large bowl, stir together the garbanzo beans, kidney beans, lemon juice and zest, tomato, onion, parsley, capers, olive oil, and salt.

Cover, and refrigerate for about 2 hours, stirring occasionally, before serving.

Makes 4 servings.

Per serving: 207 Calories; 5.5 g Protein; 20.5 g Carbohydrate; 1.5 g Sugar; 1 g Fat

Roasted Garlic (can be added to a recipe for extra flavor or mashed with olive oil for a great marinade)

- 2 heads of garlic
- Olive oil to drizzle over garlic

Heat oven to 400° F.

Slice off the top each head of garlic and expose the cloves inside.

Place the heads on a piece of foil and drizzle with olive oil.

Then wrap in the foil.

Roast until cloves are lightly browned and tender, about 30 minutes.

You can do so much with roasted garlic:

- A twist to your classic hummus is always great! Combine the roasted garlic with your beans, lemon juice, tahini, and olive oil for a new kick.
- Add your roasted garlic to sautéed spinach and cauliflower rice with some thyme for a great side dish.
- Roasted garlic is a great addition to a healthy cauliflower crust pizza. Add fresh sliced tomatoes, basil, arugula, and black olives for a completely satisfying dish.
- Create your own roasted garlic–infused olive oil! Roast your garlic and add to a pretty jar of olive oil with spices and flavor of your choice (rosemary is always a hit).

Chia Pudding

Basic Chia Pudding Base

- ¼ cup organic chia seeds
- 1 cup coconut or almond milk
- 1–2 tablespoons honey or maple syrup
- 1 teaspoon pure vanilla extract

You can go nuts with this recipe.

1–2 Tablespoon(s)

- Cacao Powder
- Pure Vanilla
- Pumpkin Puree
- Spices, etc.

Mix all ingredients (if you like the chia seeds smaller you can blend at this point) then cover and refrigerate overnight.

Makes 1 serving.

Per serving: 291 Calories: 13 g Protein; 27 g Carbohydrate; 6 g Sugar; 14 g Fat

Egg and Avocado Spaghetti Squash Boats

NOTE: If you have a fairly large spaghetti squash, you may need to increase the amount of filling you use to mix with the squash.

> ### CLEAN CUT SQUASH HINT!
> Poke some holes with a knife into the squash and put in microwave for a few minutes at a time until the squash softens a bit for easier cutting! (Save a finger!)

- 1 small spaghetti squash
- ¼–½ cup fresh salsa
- A handful greens
- 1 avocado, chopped and divided
- 2 large eggs
- Optional spices (crushed red pepper, chili lime seasonings at your local grocer, etc.)

Preheat oven to 400°F.

See note about cutting squash above. Cut spaghetti squash in half lengthwise and scoop out the seeds. Place cut side down on a sprayed baking sheet and bake for about 30 minutes. Remove from the oven and let cool until safe to the touch, about 15 minutes.

Increase the oven temperature to 425° F.

In a bowl, mix fresh salsa, 2 eggs, greens, and any spices you like. Mix thoroughly. Fork the spaghetti squash out of the shells and mix with the salsa. Fork the squash mixture back into the shells and top with avocado.

Bake for 20–25 minutes, or until the egg is cooked through.

Makes 2 servings.

Per serving: 277 Calories; 10.5g Protein; 26.5 g Carbohydrate; 9 g Sugar; 17 g Fat

Tomatillo Rotisserie Chicken

- 1 rotisserie chicken
- ½ small onion
- 1 jar tomatillo sauce (also called salsa verde)
- 3 plum tomatoes
- ¼ cup pine nuts, toasted
- 1 head broccoli, cut into small florets, steamed
- 1 avocado, diced
- 1 lime

In a medium bowl, combine chicken, onion, tomatillo, tomatoes, and pine nuts.

Add steamed broccoli.

Top with diced avocado and a squeeze of lime.

Serve with remaining avocado and lime wedges.

Can be served hot or cold.

Makes 8 servings.

Per serving: 307 Calories; 40 g Protein; 10 g Carbohydrate; 3.25 g Sugar; 11 g Fat

CHAPTER 12

Eating Out, Party Planning, and Travel

When a social event or travel is on your calendar, we want you to focus on the main themes of this book: preparation and awareness.

Eating Out the Clean Cut Way

These days, most restaurants have their menu posted online. Take a peek, decide what you are going to eat, and stick with the plan. For example, if you are not prepared going into the restaurant, your mind may switch to, "Whatever, it's one night out. I am going to have the Bolognese." Of course, there is a time and place for your cheat meals, but if this is not in your plan, the result is guilt.

A few more tips:

- Order your dressings on the side.
- Stay away from cream sauces.
- Switch your complex carb for extra vegetables.
- Drink water between your clean drinks.
- No bread.

- Use the Clean Cut three-bite dessert rule. Take three bites, tops, and put the fork down.
- Save your carbs and sugars the day before and of for that glass (or two) of wine

Party Tips for Clean Eating (You are in control.)

- Know what you are walking into.
- Drink water and eat a healthy meal BEFORE you go.
- Make your wine a spritzer or drink water between each drink (or as much as possible).
- Instead of having four or five of those "mini hot dogs," have just one.
- Try to stick with the veggie platter.
- Make the party about being with friends and family, not about the food.
- Make something that you can eat and bring!

Travel

Day of Travel:

Car, plane, train, whatever it is, you have the control to prepare before you leave. Make your bag of nuts or grab an apple, hard-boiled egg, sprouted/rye bread with almond butter, approved protein bar (like an RX bar or any simple all natural ingredient bars on the market today) or protein powder or cut-up veggies with a to-go hummus container. These are all good snacks to take on the go.

Clean eating is not a fad; even the airports have plenty of healthy options. It's here to stay.

Vacation Plans:

There is room for enjoyment, but there is no need for gluttony. There never is! Start slow, keep breakfast light, keep lunch clean, and enjoy a nice dinner but don't finish your plate. And remember the three-bite rule.

On vacation, you have more time, so use it and be active! See what your destination offers. For example, hiking, biking, sailing, paddleboarding, and kayaking are all fun activities. Maybe you will find a new hobby.

Check to see if your resort has fitness classes or daily activities as well. On your final day of vacation, enjoy. Enjoy that breakfast, that lunch, and that dinner.

Business

This is not pleasure, but it can be social. Most hotels have mini-fridges for your room if you ask. You can stock up on healthy snacks and keep them fresh. Get up a little early, take a walk or jog and check out the fitness room. In that social business, such as a conference where there is a buffet of food, make smart choices. For example, take a big portion of salad, and some fruit or yogurt. Stay away from the breads and cookies. Stick with water and use the same tips as going out to dinner. Don't be afraid to whip out a bag of nuts, a protein bar, or your protein powder which you can easily add water to. The same rules apply when eating out and socializing for business as stated above in party tips and eating out.

CHAPTER 13

Clean Cut Fitness & Nutrition Workout Examples

BEGINNER BODYWEIGHT WORKOUT

10 reps 5 rounds of each

Squats

Dips

Lunge

Plank Jack

REP: How many repetitions you do of each exercise

ROUND: A full circuit of all the exercises

After each round perform this ab set:

Crunch

Toe Reach

Bicycles

INTERMEDIATE BODYWEIGHT WORKOUT

1 minute of each exercise for 3 rounds

Squats

Push-Up

Lunge

Plank Jack

After each round perform this ab set:

Sit-ups

V-Ups

Bicycles

ADVANCED BODYWEIGHT WORKOUT

SET 1: 3 rounds of 10 reps

Burpees

Jump Squats

Push-Up with a Side Plank Rotation

Switch Lunge Jumps

Set 2: 2 rounds of 15 reps

Burpees

Jump Squats

Push-Up with a Side Plank Rotation

Switch Lunge Jumps

Set 3:1 round of 20 reps

Burpees

Jump Squats

Push-Up with a Side Plank Rotation

Switch Lunge Jumps

After each set perform this ab set 30 seconds of each

Up Down Planks

Hip Rolls

Russian Twist

You can find video samples of these exercises
at www.cleancutfit.com/bookclub

CHAPTER 14

Putting It All Together: The Clean Cut Way of Life

Thank you all for taking this journey and trusting in us. Your six weeks is coming to an end, but this new lifestyle is just beginning. This is not a diet, it is a way of life. The longer you put it into practice, the more second-nature it becomes. You will look back in a year and realize how different your mindset is about food if you keep on this journey. Remember it's about real food. There are no shortcuts and ways to trick your body or mind. It's about changing your view, not fighting it.

You know the keys to success like PREP and PLANNING but please don't forget to PAUSE, if even for a minute. It can make all the difference. Pausing allows you to see and feel what is really in front of you. The simple pause can change your outcome for the rest of the day. Take a moment for yourself, regroup then make a better choice. It's not about control, it's about the pause. If we think this way, we will stay the path. No one can be in control all the time.

Mindfulness...we say it a lot because it's another tool to make you aware of your actions. The more you are aware of triggers, choices, and patterns, the easier it is to prepare for them so when you are faced with a choice, you have planned your course of action. If you just knee-jerk to situations, you will most likely regret your decision.

Balance is what we are striving toward. We want you to enjoy the things you love but in moderation. We want to celebrate life, and food is part of that. Being kind to yourself means eating clean but also indulging in the things you enjoy. If you are too strict with yourself, it will lead to failure. Cheat and don't beat yourself up, you have the tools now to pull it back together. Slip don't fall! Remember there is always another cheat around the corner; you don't need to get it all in at one time.

This chart can help you week by week to plan and succeed! Remember, you can always access it on our book club website for a printable version.

Clean Cut Fitness & Nutrition

Weekly Prep and Guide to Success

Date: _____

Weekly Goal: _____

_____

Workouts: _____

1. _____

_____

2. _____

_____

3. _____

_____

4. _____

_____

5. _____

_____

Grocery List:

_____   _____

_____   _____

_____   _____

_____   _____

Important events and activities this week that you need to plan around:

_____

_____

GO-TO snacks and meals for the week:

_____

_____

New recipe of the week:

_____

_____

_____

_____

You have learned what to eat, when to eat, and how much. Now trust yourself, and as always, reach out. We are always right here.

You have access to our private book club page on our website. You can access grocery lists, PDFs containing week-by-week guides, measurement charts, and additional tips and recipes here:

www.cleancutfit.com/bookclub

Want to join our online community?

Visit us on Instagram and Facebook

Instagram @cleancutfitnutrition and **Facebook @cleancutfit**

We look forward to having you continue your journey with us!!

Shrink Your Body and Grow Your Mind!

Lots of love,

Lori and Caren

Made in the
USA
Middletown, DE